PURE HEART SIMPLE MIND

Wisdom stories from a life in Japan

CHARLIE BADENHOP

First Printing, 2011

charlie@seishindo.org
www.seishindo.org

ISBN 9780984823000

Published by
Seishindo
An Imprint of Arati
Helena, Montana USA

We welcome special orders of this book for educational, business,
or promotional purposes. For information regarding special orders,
please contact us at: booksales@seishindo.org

The Library of Congress has catalogued this paperback edition as follows:
Library of Congress Control Number: 2011960526

Edited by Daniel Child
Designed by Fancypants Design

To my daughter Marina,
Who brings love to my heart,
And joy to my life.
"Big love you!"

"A loving heart is the truest wisdom."

~ CHARLES DICKENS

Contents

INTRODUCTION

Pure Heart, Simple Mind, is very much a part of Japanese tradition—a tradition imbued with austerity, simplicity, subdued expression, and humility.

When creating a *bonsai*, the master prunes away all but the bare essentials, exposing a beauty that was previously obscured. When we take off our masks and share with an open heart, we illuminate our beauty and free ourselves to express our hidden truth. At such times the essence of who we are can shine through and find its rightful place in the world.

The life I have been a part of in Japan suggests that we can return to the innocence of childhood while bringing with us the wisdom we have discovered along the way. It suggests that we keep ourselves open and available to all the resources and experiences life has to offer, while gently expressing our personal truths, and striving to understand the hopes and fears of others.

You can find your connection to life—everywhere and at any time— by pausing and letting your vulnerability resonate out into the world. An open heart will lead you to the kind of experience and understanding that cuts through illusion. Follow your heart, and it will guide you to a place of acceptance and fulfillment.

MY WISH

It is my wish that in reading my simple stories, you will recognize how emotionally rewarding life can be when you open up to the people and experiences you encounter on a daily basis.

I am hoping you will feel a bond with my Japanese friends and teachers, and that you will find the stories I share with you, are in some way your stories as well. And that within these stories you can find a connection to your own heart. You will find that the simple wisdom you encounter here also resides within you!

You see, it is not my intention to write *about* Japanese people, but rather to write *through* them. To use the thoughts and feelings of my Japanese friends and teachers as a way of talking about a more universal experience that you share with them.

I want to play the role of a *nakōdo*, a matchmaker who draws people together in relationship. And thus over the course of reading this book I ask you to consider, What is the common ground all human beings share? What are the hopes and fears we all live with? What can you do to help support and nourish the many people you come in contact with?

AIKIDO

The principles of Aikido are firmly embedded in the stories I write.

Aikido is a Japanese martial art. Quite uniquely, it is a martial art that has no form of attack. No kicking, no punching, no attempt at a preemptive strike. In Aikido we engage and join with our counterparts, accepting what they offer—with the understanding that acceptance does not necessarily mean agreement.

We accept, while maintaining a safe space for all. We accept and protect both parties in the relationship. Neither agreeing nor disagreeing, we do not engage in right or wrong. Thus there is no conflict to be resolved.

I've learned to meet people in my everyday life in the same way I meet my counterparts in Aikido. Open to what they have to express and share, attempting to understand them with my heart, being careful to not try and force an outcome. Following the flow of energy expressed, and allowing this flow to take us to a generative place of deeper relationship, resolution, and rest.

FACT, OR FICTION?

My writing is both fact *and* fiction, and I want to say a bit more about this. The Japanese author Kyoko Mori once said, "I think that the best thing about being a writer is that we get to make up things and tell the truth at the same time." This is a sentiment that very much resonates with me.

In this book, rather than try to faithfully recount entire conversations, I sought to distill the essence of what was said, while adding what I felt was understood yet left unspoken. Instead of simply translating the spoken word from Japanese into English, I translated what was said through my own filter of understanding—adding some bits, and deleting others, so that you the reader would be left with only the bare essentials.

Also of great importance was that I knew it would be an important breach of privacy to use the real names and personal details of the friends I was writing about. So in many instances I changed people's names and made their true identity less clear. After all, I did not want my friends to feel I had opened up the private details of their life for all to see.

So in my writing, there is both fact and fiction, and I feel it is important that you know this starting out.

TAKE YOUR TIME, AND ENJOY YOURSELF

Travel with me to Japan, walk on the streets of my neighborhood in Tokyo, meet my teachers and neighbors, and absorb the atmosphere, energy, and vitality of the people you meet.

Breathe fully, read slowly, take in the blank space on each page, and experience an abiding sense of open-hearted friendship.

COVER CONCEPT

The wrapped stone on the cover of the book is known as a *tome ishi*, or *sekimori ishi*. The origin of these terms comes from Japanese tea ceremony, where the stone serves as 'a guardian of the path.' The stone is wrapped with reed or rope to help you realize that it was placed there by your host and that it has a message to convey.

You can find stones like this in formal Japanese gardens when you come to a fork in the path and are not sure which way to go. The stones are meant to guide you along the way, and also serve to convey the host's desire to help guests discover and walk on their spiritual path.

The stone on the cover is a symbolic invitation to open the book and follow the path within.

CHAPTERS

The book is organized into nine chapters. I've chosen a Japanese *kanji* to represent a concept expressed by the stories within each chapter. I hope you'll find the *kanji* beautiful, and perhaps somewhat mysterious as well, as you ponder how such a form of written communication came to be.

THE MEANING OF *SEISHINDO* 精心道

In my years of study and in my everyday life, I have had the opportunity to experience the importance of purity and simplicity. What I have learned along the way forms the basis for the human potential discipline I have created, called *Seishindo*.

I share an explanation here of the kanji that make up the word *Seishindo*, because the meaning of *Seishindo* is central to the concept of "Pure Heart, Simple Mind."

精

The first kanji is read 'sei'. The most basic meaning for 'sei' is "refined", but the character's meaning has been extended to include such concepts as "purity, spirit, energy, vitality, semen, excellence, and skill". In Seishindo, I have chosen the meaning "refined and pure".

心

The middle kanji is pronounced 'shin'. The meanings of 'shin' are "spirit, heart, and mind". If you ask a Japanese person where their mind is, they will point to their heart.

When we combine 'sei' with 'shin', we have the poetic expression, "pure heart, simple mind".

道

The third kanji is 'dō'. In everyday parlance it means "street, or road". As used in the Japanese arts, 'dō' means an "artful path of study"—as in Judo, Aikido, Chado (tea ceremony), and Shodo (calligraphy).

精心道

Seishindo is thus "an artful path for discovering your pure heart, simple mind".

CHAPTER 1

BEGINNING

ABOUT THE KANJI

KI (oki) - START, LAUNCH, AWAKE, RISE, INITIATE

*The two components of this kanji are "run"走
and "snake, serpent, self"乙. Snakes are cold-
blooded animals that cannot move until they have
been warmed by the rays of the sun. So when
thinking of this kanji in my mind's eye I envision
a young snake being told by its mother to get up
and get going. The youngster replies, "I have no
intention of getting up until I feel the warmth of
the sun shining on me." Many times as a child
I told my mother something similar!*

STRENGTH IN VULNERABILITY

Living in Japan for so long, I've learned a great deal about life from a unique perspective. One of my greatest teachers was my wife's grandmother, who passed away several years ago.

My most enduring memory of Obaa-chan (the Japanese term of address for grandmother) is the first time I went to her house to meet her. She was 81 years old at the time, and still rather spry. My wife rang the bell, and Obaa-chan called out for us to enter. Just as we opened the door, Obaa-chan was sliding down onto her hands and knees to bow. There was something magical and mysterious about this moment. Meeting someone for the very first time, but initially only getting the slightest glimpse of their face. As Obaa-chan descended into her bow, I was left looking at the back of her head, with her hair immaculately fashioned into a bun.

As funny as it might seem, the first thought that sprang to mind was a scene from my childhood. A teacher was lecturing me on how to best prepare when meeting an important person. He said, "If time is limited as two men prepare to meet their potential boss, the man looking to show off will spend most of his time polishing the front of his shoes until they sparkle. He does this to impress his potential boss from the moment he enters the room. The more thorough man, on the other hand, will put just as much time and attention into polishing the back of his shoes as he does the front. He does this because he realizes the importance of taking care of every detail. He values substance more than flash.

"If you take a moment to think about it, it's the thorough man that will make the best impression as he leaves the room, because he looks as good going out as he did coming in. The show-off with the scruffy heels will leave the impression of a careless man who values image more than substance."

I thought about this lesson as I looked at the back of Obaa-chan's head, as she paused with her face about six inches above the floor. She had certainly taken the time to attend to every detail!

To be standing there while a person offers their complete supplication was a totally new experience for me, and my next thought led me to consider the importance of this ritual in a culture that's been strongly influenced by the code of the samurai. Going down to one's hands and knees to bow would offer an adversary the chance to lop off one's head! I smiled as I held this thought, and realized that her show of humility also meant she was asking for my kindness. I had the feeling that by displaying her vulnerability she had somehow left me at a disadvantage! Even though I had yet to really see her face and knew almost nothing about her, I already felt I had to find a way to live up to the respect she was showing me.

Feeling suspended in space and time as I bowed sheepishly, I wondered what else I should be doing as I waited for her to complete this ritual. In that moment I remembered the words of my Aikido *sensei*. "If you want to truly know the mind of your counterpart, show them your vulnerability."

NURTURING A "PROBLEM"

The street I live on in Tokyo is so narrow that cars can barely make it past. Because of this everyone parks their bikes on one side of the street.

As instructed when moving in, my wife, my daughter, and I park our bikes across the narrow street in front of our neighbor's house. Their house sits just 21 inches back from the curb. (I actually measured!) This means they can lean slightly forward from the edge of the street, and insert their key into the lock of the front door. Such are the tight quarters that people live in here in Japan!

A few years ago, a hardy looking weed began growing next to where I park my bike. You might think such an event is barely worth mentioning, but let me explain, because initially I didn't think it was a big deal either.

The weed started life in a humble manner, sprouting out from a crack between the street and the curb. At first there didn't seem to be a reason to pull it out, and at the time I even marveled at its pioneering spirit.

It grew quite rapidly from day one, and after about six months it was beginning to look more like a tree than a weed.

Soon, birds were resting on its branches and depositing bird droppings on my bicycle seat. After having wiped away the mess several times, I finally took out my pruning shears and cut the weed-tree down.

"Sorry little guy," I said prior to lopping it off a few inches above ground level, "but you're taking up way too much space on this narrow street."

And that was the end of that!

Or so I thought …

My first mistake was ignoring the weed-tree in the first place. My second mistake was not taking a more drastic approach to getting rid of it, because it grew back as if on steroids!

In no time it had more branches than before, and the base coming out of the crack was more formidable looking. Within four months from my first attempt to cut it down, birds were once again leaving their calling cards on my bicycle seat!

This time around I had to borrow a special tool from a neighbor, and I cut the weed-tree down so that nothing at all was sticking up above the curb.

I must say I had a sense of "Good riddance!" when my work was done this time.

Well I think it was the very next morning, or two days at the most, when I noticed the hardy little son of a gun was once again sprouting new growth! I marveled at its will to live, and I began to concede a shift in the balance of power. Regardless of my tools, my supposed intelligence, and my dislike for the bird droppings, this little weed-tree was not to be deterred!

Somewhat embarrassed that it should take me so long, but I now realized there was only one viable course of action—Respect the plant and its life force, and stop thinking of it as a nuisance.

I made room for my courageous friend by moving my bike into my tiny yard. Next, I purchased some plant food and began feeding and watering the tree. I must say, the little beauty grew quite gloriously! Soon I began to lovingly trim it like a *bonsai*, and now, several years later, it's looking truly magnificent.

I find this little tree's determination to live truly inspiring. The more it was harshly treated the more it flourished. The more it's life hung in the balance, the greater its will to live. I can only hope the same is true for you and me!

EVERYTHING JUST AS IT SHOULD BE

Tokyo has countless short, narrow streets that form an intricate maze. Whenever I go rollerblading, I love to explore such unfamiliar territory.

I recently found myself in an interesting labyrinth of backstreets. In a neighborhood that seemed to have fallen asleep a number of years ago, I came upon a small nursery that sold *bonsai*. "Open 24 hours a day, seven days a week!" a sign proclaimed out front.

"Wow," I thought, "even in Japan, there's no way *bonsai* are that much in demand!"

As I rolled to a stop I saw an elderly man in the back of the yard who appeared to be sleeping sitting up. But to my surprise, he opened his eyes the moment he sensed my presence, looking wide awake and alert.

"Good day!" I called out. "Mind if I come in and have a look?"

"Please do," he said. "Would you like a cup of tea as well?"

While he prepared my tea, I found out that the shopkeeper's name was Morikawa, and that he was 78 years old. Sipping my tea, I asked how he happened to have a nursery in such an out of the way location.

"By the time I was 35 years old," he replied, "I had three children and had taken over my father's cut flower and *bonsai* shop in a fashionable part of Tokyo.

"I had a lot of money coming in, a lot of money going out, and very little free time to do anything except work. Besides missing the time I couldn't spend with my family, I had an itch to study Zen that left me feeling very restless.

"At the age of 40, I realized if I sold my shop and bought the property you're sitting in now, I'd greatly reduce my expenses. By needing less,

I could afford to want less. By simplifying my life, I could provide for my family while also leaving myself with the time to pursue my dream."

"All this sounds wonderful," I said. "But how come your sign says you're open for business 24/7? It makes you sound busy!"

"Ah," he said, "the sign is meant as a joke.

"My business is largely run on trust and appreciation, and there's no need for me to be present in order for business to be conducted.

"I know most of my clients, and they appreciate the style of my work. When I begin a new piece I usually have a particular client in mind. When I'm done, I call my client and suggest he stop by and have a look. I then take off, visiting temples and looking for interesting stock in countryside nurseries."

"Fascinating," I said. "But don't you ever worry about thieves?"

"People don't steal *bonsai*," he said with a chuckle. "Even in Japan, a thief wouldn't see the value in it. Besides, people can't imagine stealing something that seems to be there for the taking.

"We're sitting here among lots of valuable pieces of my work. I believe the best way to protect it is by not keeping it locked up.

"Having nothing to protect, I have no worry of losing anything, and everything is just as it should be.

"If you simplify your life you'll have the time to come sit *zazen* with me. I'm sure we'll soon become good friends."

Morikawa-san's eyes were soft and gentle, his smile so inviting.

OLD JAPANESE HOUSES

About a month after arriving in Tokyo I began to share an old wooden house with a group of four other *gaijin*. With the house scheduled for demolition in two years' time, the incredibly cheap rent we paid was largely a reflection of its poor condition. Living in Tokyo and only paying a hundred bucks a month in rent was something I never thought possible.

During December and January in Tokyo, it's not unusual for the thermometer to dip below freezing. In this house, I had my own way of checking the temperature on winter mornings. I pulled back the curtain and gauged the thickness of the ice on the rattling single pane window in my room. With no insulation and old houses purposely designed to allow for a free flow of air, when it was cold outside, it was also cold inside!

Another small winter inconvenience was the total lack of central heating. Central heating is a concept that has yet to warm the Japanese heart. I always chuckle when I'm outside Japan and someone remarks, "My goodness, the Japanese have heated toilet seats. What an extravagance!" My usual reply being, "With no heat in the hallways or toilet during winter, a heated seat is not nearly as extravagant as you might think!"

Nowadays housing has improved dramatically, but there's still no central heating. Back in the day, most people had kerosene space heaters warming various rooms in their house. This was not a solution anyone cared for, but in old wooden houses electric heaters were considered too dangerous.

Our house had four tiny bedrooms on the second floor. My bedroom measured nine feet long and five feet across, and I was thankful to not have many possessions at the time.

We had one very small room with a porcelain squat toilet. Getting to do numerous deep knee bends every day helped all of us stay in good shape.

No one had to wait in line in the morning to brush their teeth, because we didn't have a bathroom sink. We brushed our teeth in the kitchen, the same room we took a shower in.

You see, since the house didn't have a shower when it was first built, previous tenants had made their own. There was a door in the kitchen leading out to a tiny back yard. The entry way by the door was about two feet by two feet, and roughly six inches lower than the main floor of the kitchen. Normally, this was where you were meant to take off your shoes before coming in, but in our house this entrance space was magically transformed into a shower stall! You turned on the water as you would when washing dishes, and then rotated a cutoff valve to send water up, over, and around to a makeshift shower head attached to the wall just above the door. Since there was no drain, what you'd do was shower until the water built up and was about to overflow onto the kitchen floor. Then you'd open the door and sweep the water outside with a small broom.

As I was taking a shower one winter evening the kerosene delivery man came round to the back of the house to deliver fuel. He knocked once on the kitchen door and opened it without waiting for a reply. There I stood facing him, with my hair all lathered up and my eyes closed to keep the soap out. I can't tell you who was more surprised, but I can tell you he never entered our house again unless he heard one of us clearly invite him in!

Such was my early life in Japan. Simple, adventurous, and filled with many surprises.

WHAT DISTURBANCE?

It was six o'clock in the evening and the train platform was crowded.

I had been to the convenience store in the station, having bought two sandwiches and a packet of juice for myself, and a small box of chocolate covered almonds for my daughter, who was waiting for me at home.

As I threaded my way through the crowd, people jostled for a small plot of real estate where they could stand quietly and wait for the train. Suddenly, I noticed a commotion that was beyond the usual pushing and shoving.

A man who appeared to be homeless was pushing people as they walked past him, telling them to mind their manners. I stopped to watch as a couple of young guys made fun of the man, and then I heard someone call the police on their cell phone, saying there was a violent man on the platform. I immediately felt bad for this guy, and I knew a confrontational meeting with the police and some time in jail was not what he really needed.

I walked directly towards the man while not looking straight at him, and I could see him preparing to shove me aside. Just before reaching him, I made believe I tripped and I dropped my plastic bag, Talking to myself in English about being so clumsy, I bent over to pick up my bag, and when I stood up I was face to face with the gentleman, about one foot away.

Continuing on in my best English, I made a comment about the weather, while opening my bag to show the guy the goodies inside. Next, I motioned to a railing that was nearby, suggesting with my hands that we go stand over there. Well, not only did the homeless man get my message, but so did everyone else, as they made room for us to pass.

When we got to the railing, I pulled out a sandwich, opened the wrapping, and handed the man half, while immediately beginning to eat the other half. The man stuffed the sandwich into his mouth and wolfed it down in record time.

I opened the second sandwich, gave him half, and held onto the other half. Once again he stuffed the food into his mouth and quickly devoured it. I then gave him the remaining half, and noticed that he ate somewhat more slowly this time.

The police came along just as I was handing the man the packet of grape juice with a plastic straw sticking out. I could see they were a bit confused because there wasn't anyone acting in a violent manner. I looked over at them and said in Japanese, "Everything is fine. The man is a friend of mine. He was hungry, and therefore a bit grumpy. Now that I've fed him everything in OK. The police looked perplexed. I smiled at them, bowed a tiny bit, and thanked them for having come. Not sure what else to do, they nodded their heads in return, looked around, and then slowly walked off.

My train was just arriving, and I motioned to the man that I needed to go. He bowed deeply, stuck out his hand and said "Thank you" in English.

I handed him the box of almonds and the empty plastic bag and quickly boarded the train. As the doors closed I turned to look back and there was my new friend, bobbing up and down, bowing and smiling broadly.

I smiled back at him, but there was no room for bowing in the crowded train.

As we pulled away from the platform, I wondered what my daughter would say when I told her she had already shared all her candy with someone she had never met.

CHAPTER 2

CONSTANT

ABOUT THE KANJI

JŌ(tsune) - CONSTANT, ALWAYS, NORMAL, USUAL

*In an ever changing fast paced world, it's important
to have something constant you can depend on.
A loved one who supports you through thick or thin,
a friend you can call late at night, a set of beliefs
that are unshakable.
The more some things change, the more other
things need to stay the same.*

A SIMPLE FRIENDSHIP

My neighbor Suzuki-san, took great joy in walking her ailing Chihuahua 'Pon-chan' around the neighborhood. When Pon-chan suddenly died one day Suzuki-san was deeply saddened.

I wanted to cheer her up, so I had my daughter write a note in Japanese that read, "I'm looking forward to seeing you happy again!" I left the message and a box of cookies by her door.

The next day as I was riding away on my bicycle I saw Suzuki-san cleaning up her yard, and let out a hearty "Good morning!"

When I later returned home, she was unlocking the door to her house. She turned and asked, "Did you leave me cookies and a note yesterday?"

"Cookies and a note?" I asked. "Was the note in English?"

"No," she said, "The note was in Japanese."

"Oh, but you know I can't write in Japanese. The cookies must have come from someone else."

"Of course," she said. "I should have thought of that."

I told her I was glad to see her and that when she was in the mood I would be happy to share some of her cookies with a cup of tea.

She invited me in on the spot, and we had a lovely conversation as she showed me numerous photos of her beloved Pon-chan.

I asked her if she was thinking of getting another dog. "No," she said, "the heartbreak of losing another pet would just be too much."

Two days later when I came back home in the evening, there was a beautifully wrapped box next to my door. Inside the box was a container of my favorite tea. The note attached to the gift was written in English. It said, "Thanks so much for all your kindness!"

Since the note was in English and since Suzuki-san could neither speak nor write English, there was no way I could ask if the tea came from her without admitting that the cookies had indeed come from me.

How clever my neighbor was! She knew I wouldn't ask, and she knew I would be touched by the playful secret we now shared. It took all I had to not laugh the next time we met!

Such is the beauty of a simple friendship.

Both of us knowing what the other one felt,

And both of us expressing our friendship,

At a time when words can be too much.

A subtle gesture of solidarity,

Has a gentle yet certain ability,

To touch the heart of a friend.

HARD WORK AND FRUGALITY— TWO PILLARS OF A HAPPY LIFE

There's a shop in my neighborhood that does laundry and ironing that I've been using for more than twenty-five years now. Over time the master and I have become friends, though I do need to emphasize 'over time'. Ishibashi-san works such long hours that it was hard to get the opportunity to talk with him.

You see, there was something about his smile and tone of voice when he welcomed people into his shop that led me to want to know him better. But he was always busy ironing clothing, and I didn't want to interrupt his work flow. So I had to create a strategy that would induce him to take a few minutes to talk.

I bought two cans of ice cold beer on a hot summer evening, and dropped by his shop just before closing to pick up a shirt I had left with him.

"Would it be bad manners," I asked, "if I offered you a can of ice cold beer?"

"Well no, it wouldn't be," he said. "if you wouldn't mind my opening up a package of squid for the two of us to snack on."

And thus the conversation began!

"We only work six days a week now," he said. "but for about thirty years after World War II, my wife and I worked seven days a week, usually at least fourteen hours a day. We got up 4 a.m. every morning, had a simple breakfast if there was enough food, and worked until late at night. We took one five day vacation a year. We were happy to have the work, because the work allowed us to have a constant source of food and shelter, and the work made it possible for us to afford having two children.

"When you spend so much time working, you don't have the time to worry about the future. The more free time people have, the more selfish

22

and self-indulgent they tend to become. I must say, I look at young people today and I'm not surprised that Japan is having so many problems. My parents taught me the importance of frugality and hard work, and I find these principles to be two of the pillars of a happy life. When people had less they complained less. When people lived within their means, they were much less afraid of losing what they had. Nowadays so many people are frantic and worried, and few people have the time to truly nurture their family.

"The trouble these days is that people build a lifestyle they can't easily support. If they lost their high paying job and had to work in a laundry like mine, they would feel like their life had collapsed. Their children would be devastated that they could no longer buy the next generation of game console. People have lost touch with the essentials, and they've lost touch with the value of hard work. Hard work is the glue that keeps your life together.

"One more important point is this," he said. "I think any job where you sit all day, weakens your spirit. I sit when I eat and lay down when I sleep, but other than that I stand and move all day. Standing and moving makes you strong and builds your resilience to adversity. When you stand, you use your whole self, and thus you feel more in control of your life. My father worked until he was 73 and I'm already 79 and still going strong. I want to die standing up, rather than live my life sitting down. Easier is not better!"

BIRDWALKING

You may recall that I wrote earlier about my friend Suzuki-san, whose beloved dog had died.

Well, one day about a year later, I noticed Suzuki-san walking with a caged parakeet. At first I wondered what she was doing. Perhaps she had been taking care of someone's bird while they were away, and was now returning the little creature to it's rightful owner?

My answer came a few days later. Turning the corner on my way home, I literally bumped into Suzuki-san, and she promptly took our chance encounter as an opportunity to introduce me to her new friend, Pepe. As it turned out, the bird she was walking with was her new pet.

She told me of the bird's special lineage, and pointed out in great detail how finely feathered little Pepe was. After a very thorough introduction, with me bowing to Pepe, and Pepe's cage bobbing up and down in return, she asked for my good will in welcoming him into the neighborhood!

"Oh," I said, "if Pepe ever needs anything at all, I hope he won't hesitate to ask!"

I offered my best wishes to Suzuki-san and Pepe and bowed once more before leaving to cook dinner for my daughter. Thus, a new relationship was born.

Little by little Pepe and I became the best of friends. You see, Suzuki-san took to walking Pepe several times a day, and since she always enjoyed talking to her foreign friend Charlie, she tended to walk Pepe at a time of day when she was fairly certain that I would be either leaving or returning home.

It's one thing to meet a neighbor on the way out and simply call out "Hello!" as you pass by. It's something else again when you are rushing to catch a train or meet someone, and your neighbor wants to chat about her friend. You would have to be awfully impolite to not stop and listen. So, when pressed for time, I took to leaving a few minutes earlier than usual, as otherwise I knew that Suzuki-san and Pepe would most likely be waiting.

Suzuki-san was impressed that Pepe responded to my English in much the same way as he did when she spoke Japanese to him. Indeed, she wondered aloud more than once about how intelligent Pepe must be in order to have bilingual comprehension skills.

"Just think" she said, "I had six years of English in school and I can barely understand a word you say when you speak English to me. Pepe on the other hand, hasn't had any schooling whatsoever, and he understands you better than I do!"

Somehow it was hard to argue with her logic.

Though, when I think about it, Pepe was not all that talkative in either Japanese or English. Not that it mattered. Suzuki-san was happy to do the talking for him.

NEVER UNDERESTIMATE THE POWER OF YOUR ORIGINAL SELF

In writing this book I had a lot of conversations with a lot of people and I scribbled a lot of notes on paper napkins and in the margins of books. Some of what I collected just did not fit into a story, but were concepts that I still wanted to share. What follows is a series of wise statements, spoken by my friends and teachers.

We increase our suffering by failing to appreciate the opportunities and learning our current challenges offer us. There is no life without challenges.

When we attempt to escape from what we find unpleasant, we miss out on learning life-affirming lessons and achieving what we most desire. Attempting to move away from what we do not want leads us to settle for the scraps of life, instead of feasting on the meal.

Indeed the more you try to avoid suffering, the more suffering you will wind up experiencing. The same is true of illness.

You will improve the quality of your life by striving to better understand what it is that confuses you, rather than looking to escape from your turmoil.

'Solution' and 'problem' are two sides of the same coin. With a solution in hand, there is no problem. Look for the solutions inherent in your current situation, rather than looking to fix what you perceive to be wrong.

Instead of fighting against the seeming competing desires you have, use your whole self to stay cooperatively engaged in your struggle and you will find something within you shifts Over time your struggle will be transformed into a life-affirming lesson.

Wanting to experience peace of mind is a fine goal to have, if you also realize you will sometimes have little choice but to feel distressed. In fact, much of life happens in between the two.

Nothing stays the same forever and thus change is inevitable. Today's suffering will turn into tomorrow's happiness, and eventually you will surely suffer once again. That is just the way life is.

Accepting that change is inevitable helps you move *with* life rather than attempting to hold onto either the 'bad' or the 'good'. As you open up to the need for change, you will find yourself suffering more effectively. Peace of mind is sure to follow!

In Aikido we understand that if we follow the direction of an attack without impeding the attacker, the confusion being expressed will be fully expended and a new, more life-affirming relationship can then begin to emerge.

You need some silence and solitude in your life so that you can begin to hear the inner voice of your original self. This is not the voice of your internal dialogue. This is the voice that is hidden in the depths of your soul, and it speaks to you without words.

It is your internal chaos that destroys your capacity for inner peace, and not the world around you. It is your internal chaos that weakens the root energy of your life force and the wisdom of your original self. You need to strive to know yourself as you were in the beginning of your life. Know yourself as you were as a very young child—filled with amazement and curiosity.

A happy life is not built upon understanding why. A happy life requires that you live in the midst of uncertainty and do so gracefully. When you are graceful there is a beauty that exudes from the way you move and carry yourself, because you do only what is necessary. Nothing more and nothing less. When you are graceful there is a sense of proper proportion—an ideal relationship—between yourself and the rest of life, between your happiness and your sadness. You sense your life is 'just right' as it is, and thus there is a stillness that permeates your being, in the midst of the unknown.

When you experience grace in the midst of illness, defeat, or other suffering, you're able to appreciate the small pleasures of life, and each challenge you face serves to strengthen the dreams you hold in your heart.

CHAPTER 3

BEAUTY AND PERFECTION

ABOUT THE KANJI

BI (utsuku) - BEAUTY, GRACE, CHARM, VIRTUE

*In Japanese culture, truth is considered to be more
important than beauty,
At times, however, a natural, pure beauty can help
lead one to a deep sense of truth.*

CULTIVATING BEAUTY, CULTIVATING LOVE

Living in Japan, I'm amazed by the *bonsai* displays of local people who keep their collections as a hobby. One of my favorites is a treasure trove of about one hundred chrysanthemums sitting in the yard of an elderly gentleman. Some of the plants stand close to five feet tall and have one massive bloom each. Other varieties are short and dense, and have been shaped to look like colorful clouds.

Over the past few years I had strolled by my neighbor's garden on many occasions, and yet in all that time he never once looked up from his plants, so intent was he on his work.

While out for a stroll one day, I noticed the flowers looking more robust than ever. My neighbor was bent over inspecting the leaves of a large, blooming chrysanthemum, and I decided to finally strike up a conversation.

"Hello!" I called out. "Your chrysanthemums look lovely this season!"

The old man straightened up quickly, looking to see who was calling out to him. Soon we were talking as if we were old friends.

Ueda-san said he was 81 years old and had been tending his flowers for thirty-five years. I asked him what motivated him to take on such an ambitious project. He told me he started shortly after his son was killed in an auto accident.

"The beauty of the flowers," he said, "reminded me of the warmth of my son's smile. By tending the flowers, I felt I was continuing to cultivate the love I felt for him."

I was deeply touched by his words and stood there in silence, not knowing what to say.

"You see," he continued after a while, "the flowers helped me appreciate that even though I was feeling very sad, there was still great beauty in the world. By recognizing and responding to that beauty, I was keeping my heart open to life.

"Now I realize that life has much to offer me, both good and bad. My flowers taught me that it's important to balance my sorrow by cultivating my joy. Without my flowers, I would have lost the sense that there is beauty in the world. In trimming my plants, I play a small role in helping life express its beauty."

Sensing our time together was complete for today, I bowed and offered my thanks.

As I continued on my way, it occurred to me that by nurturing our relationships we nurture ourselves. By cultivating the beauty we see in others, we also cultivate love. In this case, the beauty and love Ueda-san had been cultivating in his flowers for so many years was reaching out and touching the hearts of his neighbors.

PERFECTION AND IMPERMANENCE

During my many years in Japan I've taken the opportunity to dabble in various Japanese arts. I always come away feeling inspired by the sensitivity and attention to detail that is expressed.

One of my explorations led me to take a few lessons in *ikebana*, the art of Japanese flower arrangement. During my brief training my teacher told me the following.

"In contrast to the clustering of numerous blooms typical in Western flower arrangements, *ikebana* is usually characterized by a line of twigs or leaves, connected by a sparse arrangement of flowers, the idea being to give viewers the sense that they have just come across a scene in nature.

"In *ikebana* one of the branches in an arrangement is often bent or broken. This signifies the practitioner has attempted to present the arrangement in a 'natural' state. It is the 'imperfection' of the broken branch that leads us to understand the practitioner is striving to express 'perfection' as it appears in nature. The arranger hopes that in viewing the arrangement, you might come to appreciate that your own 'broken branches' are what signify your uniqueness and beauty.

"Each one of us, no matter how successful or evolved we might appear to be, has imperfections and personal ego attachments. These imperfections and attachments are not something to be overcome or transcended, but rather aspects of ourselves to be understood, appreciated, and accepted. If we do not honor and appreciate our human frailties as an essential part of who we are, we will always be attempting to eradicate some aspect of ourselves that we perceive to be lacking.

"Consider the sense of perfection and pure life force you get when holding a baby. It is the baby's uncontrived and unrestrained expression of their emotional experience that gives us a sense of life at its fullest. This is the inherent blessing we receive from the essence of life in its simplest and purest form. Rather than hoping for love or acceptance, the baby expresses who she is and what she feels in this very moment. This is the same free flow of energy that *ikebana* practitioners strive to express in their floral arrangements. We look to strip our work of any contrived sense of beauty so that the natural energy and life force of the flowers can be freely expressed and felt. In other words, we attempt to present the flowers 'as they are', rather than attempting to add anything extra. We strive to let the flowers communicate directly, and thus in some way hope to reconnect viewers to their own heartfelt sense of beauty and perfection."

At the conclusion of one lesson my teacher said, "Today, there is one more thing I would like to say. I am drawn to flower arranging because it helps me understand and come to terms with the impermanence of life. No matter how beautiful the flowers are when the arrangement is complete, I know they will only express their beauty for a few days' time. By carefully cleaning and cutting the flowers and adding water, we can extend their life for a few precious moments. But in the end you're left with the understanding that neither the flowers nor any other form of life will last forever. One of the most important things we can do in life is appreciate the beauty and perfection that is present in our lives right now, rather than lamenting the passing of life. By appreciating the fleeting beauty of the flowers, you can come to understand the fleeting beauty of your own life, and the lives of those you love."

PERFECT IMPERFECTIONS

One afternoon recently I went to a pottery shop outside Tokyo and happened to meet the head potter, who had stopped by to check on her staff.

After looking around the shop I asked the potter if she had a few minutes to chat and explain her work to me. The first thing she talked about was how a potter never knew what was going to wind up coming out of the kiln. "Each kiln opening," she said, "is somewhat like Christmas morning. Sometimes you get many wonderful gifts, and sometimes you end up with coal in your stocking. Like when most of the pieces explode in the kiln due to severe changes in weather.

"It's the element of chance," she said, "that makes the work so magical. It keeps you humble, and you learn to surrender and accept the unknown."

Next she talked to me about design and functionality—topics important to every potter. "There's no sense in having an attractive piece that is awkward to use, and there's no sense in having a boring piece that is highly functional," she said.

Since I had decided that I very much liked her work and was definitely going to buy something, I picked out three pieces to choose from. I set them on the counter and asked the lady to tell me a bit about each piece.

"By talking about these three pieces, I can explain how I appreciate desirable imperfections in my work." she said.

"Notice in this first piece how the glaze is not a consistent thickness over the inside surface. I tried my best to smooth out the glaze," she continued, "but this is a very tough glaze to work with. Still, for me it's the inconsistency of the glaze that makes this piece so interesting. In fact, that's what brings out the broad range of colors you see here."

Turning to the next piece, she continued, "With this one you'll notice that the bowl is not perfectly round. I am a small woman and this is a large piece for me to throw on the wheel. In fact, this is as big a piece as I am currently able to throw. I love making something this size because these bowls really test my limits. There is a certain tension present when the shape goes out of being fully round, and that is what draws me to this piece. I hope when people look at it they get the sense that I'm testing my limits.

"Finally," she went on, "with this third piece you'll notice the price is considerably less than the other pieces. This piece is skillfully made. In fact, I feel it's a bit 'too good' and so it looks like it could have been machine made. That's why the price is less than for the others.

"The shape is perfectly round, and the glaze flows evenly over the entire pot, and so the piece somehow lacks a sense of uniqueness. I've stopped making this shape and size because I know how to make them all too well. When they come out this perfectly I feel like the soul of the pot gets left in the kiln. It does not come across as being one of a kind."

She bowed ever so slightly and asked, "Do you have a moment? I have some locally grown strawberries, and it is always best to eat them at this time of year, while sipping a warm cup of tea."

CHAPTER 4

SELF-SACRIFICE

ABOUT THE KANJI

HOU (sasa) - SELF-SACRIFICE, DEDICATION,
DEVOTION, CONSECRATION, SERVICE

*In Japanese culture self-sacrifice and being of service
to others, are highly regarded virtues. When I am
invited to dinner, I never cease to be amazed at
how the host and hostess will eat very little until
they are sure that I have had my fill.*

*More than once, I have been lost in downtown
Tokyo and a Japanese person has come by and shown
me to my destination in the midst of a rain storm!*

LOSS—AN ESSENTIAL ELEMENT OF SUCCESS AND HAPPINESS

In my neighborhood there are a number of restaurants that cater to the same men coming in as often as five or six times a week for dinner and a drink. Such places have a family feel to them, with everyone knowing each other well. I was in such a place about a month after the big earthquake and tsunami up north of Tokyo, and as usual Kubota-san was giving his wide ranging interpretation of the nightly news.

"Now is the time for the Japanese people to show their true spirit." Kubota-san said. "You never really know the heart of another person during good times. It's not until some form of disaster that you find out what people really believe and what they base their life upon.

"In Japanese culture we are taught to celebrate success in a subdued fashion, keeping in mind that tomorrow brings a new set of challenges. We are taught that success is fleeting and doesn't last all that long.

"Over time, I think many Japanese people have come to misunderstand the meaning of success and the happiness it can bring. These days it seems people confuse success with winning or being able to say, 'I am better than others.' In my mind, nothing could be further from the truth. I believe you can't really understand success until you've tasted defeat. Loss is an essential element of success and happiness."

I nodded my head and said nothing, knowing my friend was speaking an important truth.

"You see," Kubota-san said, "I grew up as a farmer, and as a farmer you soon learn that a good crop is often followed by a bad crop the following season. Also, as a farmer you share the water used for growing your rice with all your neighbors. Because each person needs to depend on the good will of another, you can't celebrate a good harvest unless your neighbors also did well. In our rice-growing culture, we learned that water and rice are meant to be shared with the entire community.

During hard times you shared your food with your neighbors if they had none, knowing they would do the same for you.

"Now, as a nation we need to share with each other once again. Those of us with more, need to give to those who have less. It's in the act of giving that you feel your connection to others. When you give, you offer up thanks for all you have, and appreciate the fact that you don't live this life as a separate individual.

"Times like now help you realize how fleeting success and happiness are. It's only after losing everything that you can finally fully appreciate how much you had before. A healthy person tends to take their good health for granted ... until they get sick.

"These days it seems people don't really experience appreciation, because they're always wanting something more. People don't seem to know what it feels like to be satisfied. I taught my children to not base their good feeling on something that will likely be gone tomorrow. I also taught them to not base their good feeling on what they can buy.

"As you've heard me say before, I believe losing World War II was a great gift for the Japanese people. A very harsh gift, but a great gift nonetheless, because losing tested the strength of the Japanese soul. We had to reevaluate our culture and discover what this defeat really meant for us. We had to dig deep to find our hearts laying underneath the rubble of the bombings.

"And now, I fervently pray we find the courage to accept this earthquake and tsunami as another gift meant to test our spirit. I'm hoping that the coming years are a time for great renewal in Japan."

THE BENEFITS OF WORKING

Older Japanese people have a deep respect for work that has always touched me and made me reflect. They believe that money is only one of the many benefits received from working, and that it is not the most important benefit.

In my neighborhood there is a husband and wife in their seventies that have a lovely restaurant. The wife is a fantastic cook and she and her husband are always friendly and kind. I asked them recently if they had done any thinking about retiring, and it was as if I had spoken a naughty word.

"Oh, my goodness," the husband said, "what would we do if we retired? We have made many friends by serving our neighbors through the years, and we would both be very sad to not see them any more."

"Yes, indeed," the wife said. "losing touch with our customers would be sad. But the other thing," she continued, "the more important thing is that we would lose our opportunity to serve the people in our community. The reason for having this restaurant has never been simply as a means to make money. The most important reason for our having this restaurant, and perhaps the most important reason for having any job, is to be of service to the people in your community. It gives you the opportunity to not be selfish and to do something for others. There's no finer activity in life than serving others!"

As I smiled and nodded my head, I felt blessed to know these two fine people.

"You know Tabata-san, who often comes here for lunch," the wife said. "She's the janitor at the local community center. Her greatest pleasure at work is keeping the toilets spotlessly clean. She has talked about this more than once. She strives to keep the toilets so clean that everyone feels at home when needing to use them. And she takes great pride in providing this service."

"How about Shimizu-san?" the husband injected. "He came in second in the window washing competition our local area has started to have, and there was a big party here afterwards to celebrate. He takes great pride in his job, and he hopes his son will some day follow in his footsteps."

"Whatever one does, I think it's important to do it well," the wife chipped in. "To do your job to the best of your ability. When you do this you feel good about what you're doing, and so you feel good about yourself. Usually, as an extra added bonus, people will compliment you on a job well done. That leaves you with a smile on your face and feeling very satisfied.

"With all the benefits I get by working, perhaps it is a selfish activity after all," the wife said with a twinkle in her eyes. "Getting up early in the morning knowing that I have somewhere to go and something meaningful to do, helps me stay young and healthy. It's much better than staying home and using my next doctor's appointment as an excuse to get out of the house. When my first customer of the day comes in and I bow and say 'Welcome!', I know there's still a reason why I'm alive."

"Without good service the world would be a very lonely place," the husband added. "The basis for good service is respecting others. The basis for respecting others is being grateful for all you have. I would love to have the opportunity to serve a meal to the leaders of North Korea. I would say, 'Please sit and enjoy yourselves. I will do my very best to serve you well.' Regardless of the political outcome, I know on some level my message would sink in!"

MAMA-SAN

If I'm going out at night, I very much prefer the back alleys and small streets in Tokyo. My favorite establishments fit a maximum of ten customers, with a *mama-san* presiding. It's all very personal and up close, and each place has its own cast of characters.

I love the shops run by *mama-sans* because I'm fascinated to watch these ladies take charge in a man's world. It's a man's world at night because very few Japanese men take their wives out for entertainment, and very few women would walk into an old-fashioned drinking establishment on their own.

One of my all time favorite *mamas* is Kaoru-san, and one night when I was the only customer, I asked her to tell me why ladies such as her are known as '*mama*'.

She smiled warmly and said "Oh Charlie-san, I love knowing what you think about, and I'm always happy to answer your questions, as long as you don't ask me how old I am."

We both had a chuckle, and then she began to explain.

"Well" she said, "Most every *mama*, whether she's an actual mother or a shopkeeper like me, knows two important things about men.

"The first is that most every man is still a boy at heart. Because of this they enjoy telling dirty jokes and saying things to lightly shock or embarrass a woman. For instance, it's easy for everyone to see I'm small-breasted," she said as she cupped her hands around her modest breasts, "and yet many of my customers at some point tell me what splendid breasts I have. They're thrilled to be able to say such a thing without being severely scolded, and they're very much hoping what they say will fluster me.

"But I don't scold them, and I don't get flustered, and in a way I think this might leave some of them ever so slightly disappointed.

"The second thing *mamas* know is that men want to be loved even when they have been naughty or behaved badly.

"In fact it might be more accurate to say that it's after they have behaved badly that men want more than ever to be shown they're still loved.

"The few times I do get angry and let a customer know he's gone too far, it's likely he'll bring me a small gift the next time he comes in, as a way of saying he's sorry. When he does this, I might make him a special dish, just to let him know he's still part of the family.

"They call me '*mama*' because just like their real mothers, I do my best to cater to their needs. If a certain customer comes in every Wednesday night and he likes mackerel, then I do my best to have mackerel on the menu every Wednesday. If a customer happens to like fried eggplant and I don't have any eggplant on hand, then if it's not busy I'll run out and buy some. Just like their own mother might have done when they were a child. You see, in running a small shop like this, making money isn't what's important. What's important is that because my customers and I depend on each other, our relationship can be quite special. I strive to have my customers feel at home so they'll want to come back again. That's why, when they come in, I call out the same greeting that their mother used to use when they came home from school.

"I still remember the first night you came into my small shop," Kaoru said. "I will admit now that I was a bit frightened. I hadn't ever served a *gaijin* before and I wasn't sure how you would react to my simple offerings. I'm so glad that over the years we have come to be good friends."

STALKING THE TRUTH

After five years another *gaijin* finally moved into my apartment building. Like me, Jim was a New York City boy. As it turns out, he also liked to cook for a hobby.

Soon after moving in, Jim invited some new Japanese friends of his over for dinner. I was present to serve as his ally and translator, as he had only been in Tokyo for less than a month and spoke very little Japanese.

Jim planned on serving a number of different courses on small plates, along with a different wine for each course. But by the time his guests had sampled his second offering, it was clear they weren't enjoying the food. They were taking small forkfuls and washing most bites down with a bit of wine.

Jim had the same feeling as me, and being a true-to-heart New Yorker he asked me to ask what they thought of his food. I realized such a direct question would only put his friends on the spot, so instead I said, "Ah yes, this food is good. It very much reminds me of being in New York. Isn't it great?"

To which everyone mumbled a polite, "Oh yes, everything is great!"

"But," I said in somewhat of a loud voice, while pausing to add a bit of drama, "If a Japanese person knew all the basic ingredients, I'm sure they'd make this dish differently. Isn't that so?"

My intent was to give Jim's guests a safe target to aim at. Critiquing Jim's food would be impolite. But talking about how this 'great meal' would be made differently by a Japanese person, was a much easier conversation to have.

Several of the guests were already nodding their head "Yes" to my question as they looked around, each one visually imploring the others to make a comment. After a few seconds of awkward silence, Watanabe-san gathered up the courage to speak.

"Well," she said, "This dish is very good, there's no question about that. But I have no idea how to cook foreign food, so I'm very hesitant to offer any further opinion." She took a sip of her wine and looked around at her Japanese comrades. I wasn't sure if she was waiting for someone else to jump in, or if she was simply gathering the courage to continue.

Finally she said, "Well, knowing nothing about foreign cooking, I'm guessing the average Japanese would add a bit more salt and a bit less hot sauce, even if doing so would ruin the taste."

"What did she say?" Jim immediately asked.

"Pour a bit more wine and I'll gather the dishes," I said, "and then I'll meet you in the kitchen."

By the time he made it to the kitchen Jim was clearly vexed and asked, "Why couldn't you just tell me what she said?"

"Because," I countered, "if I had done so, everyone would have been embarrassed. The good news is that everyone likes the basic taste of the food. The even better news is, now you know what to do with the rest of the meal you're preparing. Add some salt, and do away with the chilli peppers."

"Jeez," Jim said, "why couldn't they just tell me the truth?!"

"Because" I replied, "They realize there is no truth to be told, but only their opinion. When faced with a choice, they'd prefer to endure the food rather than risk damaging a friendship."

"Welcome to Japan!"

SHARING THE WEALTH

A rather old man who lives in my Tokyo neighborhood came shuffling along on his way to go shopping.

He stopped and talked with a girl of around six, who was playing by herself in the parking lot of my apartment complex. It was obvious by the animated nature of their conversation that the man and the girl knew each other well.

The man asked the girl how she was doing in school. She said she was working hard, and that even though it meant less play time, she was studying a lot every day. The man praised her for her effort and exhorted her to do her best. Then he reached in his jacket pocket and pulled out a candy bar, which he offered the girl as a reward. She bowed and accepted with little hesitation. The old man smiled, bowed back to the girl, and continued on down the street.

Just as the girl began to eagerly tear off the candy wrapper her older brother and his friend came along.

Upon seeing the candy, the brother quickly decided all three of them should share in the girl's bounty, so he took the candy bar away from his sister and began to think out loud about how to split it up. He and his friend quickly started arguing over who should get what, as the girl stood there and began to cry. I was tempted to somehow intervene, but I thought it might not be wise to do so. Even though the children and I were rather friendly, I thought I might be out of place by stepping in.

The noise of the arguing boys and the crying girl drew the mother's attention, and she soon came out of her apartment to see what was going on. It didn't take her but a second to size up the situation, and she took the candy bar from her son and gave it back to her daughter.

The mother gently but sternly scolded her son. "Not only were you being mean to your sister, but you were teaching your friend bad manners as well." The son bowed to his mother, offered his apologies, and then bowed and apologized to his sister as well. The other boy was quite embarrassed and stood there staring down at the ground.

The mother squatted down and drew her daughter to her side. She asked if everything was OK now, and the girl said, "Yes."

Next, the mother said, "Even though your brother has been quite naughty, it's still better to share what you have with others, rather than keeping everything all to yourself."

Still a bit teary eyed, the girl slowly nodded her head "Yes" as she stood there with the candy bar in her hand. She asked her mother if she should give some candy to both her brother and his friend, and her mom said, "As an act of kindness it would be a very nice thing to do."

The girl divided the candy equally between herself and the two boys, even as the boys once again apologized for their bad behavior.

At that point the mother said to all three, "Go ahead and eat the candy now, before the chocolate starts to melt in your hands."

CHAPTER 5

PATIENCE, ENDURANCE

ABOUT THE KANJI

NIN (shino) - TO BEAR, TO ENDURE, STEALTH

In Japanese culture, patience, and subdued expression are important virtues. Many is the time I've heard a Japanese mother tell her child to endure a little bit longer so as to not inconvenience others. The importance of 'suffering quietly' is highly valued.

SUBMERGED IN AN ICE-COLD POND

My wife's *obaa-chan* had a spirit and wisdom that infused her stories, and made her a treasure to be around. She also had a resilience that clearly saved her life during World War II.

One evening I asked her what World War II had been like for her. Here is what she had to say.

"Much of Tokyo was destroyed by U.S. fire bombing during the end of World War II. It was very dangerous because fires would rage nightly and spread rapidly.

"It was devastating to lose one's worldly possessions and the very house you lived in, all in a few minutes' time. But it was even more devastating to hear the screams of those writhing in pain as they became trapped between fires, with no way to escape.

"The safest place to be during the fire bombings was on the grounds of a neighborhood temple. With only two buildings on the large property the bombers did not target this area. Most importantly, though, there was a large pond on the grounds. If you submerged yourself in the pond up to your chin, you could protect yourself from the flying sparks coming from the many wooden buildings on fire.

"Going in that pond every night took determination." she said. "In winter the air and water were cold. Some people didn't have the fortitude to stay in the pond until the bombers left. But staying alive was more important than comfort, so for me getting out of the pond early was not an option.

"This is how I managed. I wore several layers of clothes to help keep my body heat in. Once I got to the pond I would quickly immerse myself up to my chin. I felt it was very important to not slowly suffer through this process.

"Next," she continued, "I would look for the largest blazing fire in the distance and make believe it was one of the large fires built during one of the summer festivals. I would imagine myself getting a bit too close to the fire and needing to cool off by immersing myself in the pond. I would then look at the sparks flying everywhere and imagine they were the famous Tokyo summer fireworks display. Remembering vividly how hot it was at that time of year, it felt great to cool off in the pond."

At this point she stopped talking and we looked at each other while also looking off into the distance.

"Over the past few years on the first of January, you've come with us when we go to the temples in the old neighborhood to pray. Now you know the significance of the one temple we always visit last. While there, I give thanks for being spared and I pray for the souls of all those who departed during the bombings. Asking that their pain be erased from their souls.

"Now," she said, "we have come full circle. You are American, and you have married my granddaughter. I pray this means the suffering of World War II is being transformed into friendship and love.

"Japan is a very different country as a result of the war," she said. "Perhaps such terrible suffering was necessary to bring about such a great change."

We both sat there for awhile saying nothing. As she had told her story with such gentle intensity, the two of us had slipped off into a lovely state of reverie. It took a bit of time to travel back into the present, where we were sitting in the safety of her living room.

Powerful stories are often magical in that way.

LESSONS FROM HARD TIMES

I have many fond memories of sitting in a small room in the house of my wife's grandmother, sipping tea and giving *Obaa-chan* the space to talk. When I asked her again about World War II, here is what she had to say.

"The deaths of loved ones, natural disasters, wars, and divorces. All of these events give us cause to stop and reflect on our lives.

"World War II taught me a lot. It seems to me that in all wars, both sides tend to be correct in standing up for their values, and quite shortsighted in denying their shortcomings.

"I think this is also true in personal relationships that aren't going well. People fail to realize and acknowledge their own shortcomings, and this prevents them from recognizing that there are always two people responsible for the failing.

"When the war ended I was grateful to still be alive and I was ready to redirect my life. Having withstood the war I was pretty certain I could withstand everything life had to offer.

"Countless precious lives were lost and many died young. The war broke my heart and caused me to reexamine everything I thought I knew. I was pretty certain my heart would break a few more times before I died, and I needed to take the time to better understand how life is full of suffering *and* joy, love *and* hate.

"I found myself wondering what all the killing had accomplished. What truths had the war revealed? What lessons were to be learned by every Japanese person? Surely our culture needed to redirect itself, and I wondered how this would be accomplished, or indeed *if* it would be accomplished. Before the war life had a certain familiarity that felt comfortable. Up early every morning to start the day, working well into the evening … all with a sense of an endless rhythm and flow, with one day leading to the next. By the end of the war, everything had been turned upside down. Everyone was so busy rebuilding shattered lives and attempting to make up for lost time, that few people took the time to sit and reflect.

"I realized I was going to have to let go of great sadness in order to begin the next stage of my life. Having seen so many people die, I found it important to focus my attention on the newborn babies in our neighborhood, watching them grow and flourish under the gaze of a loving mother. Life was indeed continuing to spring forth, and I knew it was important to focus on the positive.

"The war led me to understand the world is being destroyed by the anger and resentment that is stirred up by our leaders. Beneath all the bad feelings lies a deep fear that is big enough to destroy all of life. When our fear, anger, and resentment overflow into war, they squeeze the love from our hearts. At that point, there are no winners, only survivors.

"God is the spirit that lives within each of us and gives us life. Who we are depends to a large extent on how we love. We need to nurture our fear and our anger with kindness, so that hope, health, and compassion will spring forth in each of us—regardless of the country we were born in or the values we hold dear.

"There is a great deal of fear and anger in the world today. Please consider how you can nurture with kindness all those you meet and enter into relationship with."

ENDLESS DETERMINATION

Recently someone asked what brought me to Japan in the first place. I replied that there was something about the spirit of Aikido and the austere sense of aesthetics in all the Japanese arts that fascinated me. I thought some more about this later on, and I remembered a fascinating story about Japan, I'd heard as a young man.

Many years ago there were two young boys, Kazu and Hiroo, growing up on the outskirts of Kyoto. They both loved *kyudo*, the art of Japanese archery, and while in high school they practiced as much as they could.

Upon graduating Kazu had to quit *kyudo so* that he could work in his family's business, making the protective armor worn by *samurai* during battle. The armor was heavily padded and Kazu joined the pieces together with a sewing machine that had a large wheel used to position the thick needle in the correct location for piercing the fabric. The job was physically demanding and dangerous. If Kazu's mind wandered for just a moment, he could easily pierce his hand instead of the fabric.

As the youngest of three boys, Hiroo had little in the way of family commitments. So he offered himself up as an apprentice to a renowned *kyudo* master. He eventually became known as one of the best archers in all of Japan.

When both boys had ripened to become men in their fifties, the Emperor declared a nationwide competition to honor the role and importance of Japan's many fine archers. On his way to the competition Hiroo the archer stopped by to see his childhood friend Kazu. He told his friend about the upcoming event, and Kazu sheepishly asked if he could enter the competition being introduced as Hiroo's student. Although Hiroo thought the proposal somewhat foolish, because of their strong friendship in the past, he agreed to bring Kazu along.

With all the masters and their many students present, people were expecting a great display of prowess. With two arrows to shoot, whoever pierced the target twice would be given a sizeable quantity of gold and a large plot of land. To everyone's surprise however, the target was placed at twice the distance of their everyday practice!

With the target positioned much farther away than usual, one master after another failed to hit the target with both arrows. Finally with every master having missed the mark their students were given the opportunity to shoot. In the minds of everyone there, the competition was all but over.

With no official ranking, Kazu was the very last person with a chance to shoot and win the prize. He gathered his spirit and let loose his arrows. They both flew straight and sure, piercing the target. Everyone in attendance was speechless as the Emperor presented Kazu with his lavish reward.

With the ceremony over, Hiroo rushed over to Kazu and asked, "After not practicing all these years, how in the world did you manage to hit the target both times?"

"Well," Kazu replied, "as an artisan, I aim to pierce a heavy fabric in just the right spot countless times everyday. Today, I simply imagined that the arrow was my needle, and then aimed it the same way I always do! The result was no different from what happens when I work.

"Whether in *kyudo* or at work, I've always been aiming at the same target—myself. All these years I have remained determined to fulfill my true potential. It was this determination that carried my arrows to the target today."

PAIN ... AND THE MIND OF AN UNDISCIPLINED CHILD

In Aikido we strive to find ways to leave our habits behind and experience the world from a "simple mind" perspective. A task that is much easier said than done.

We do things like sitting in *seiza* for an hour at a time. With our legs folded underneath us it doesn't take but five or ten minutes before we start feeling pain in our legs and knees.

After twenty minutes the pain is excruciating, and we're quite sure we won't be able to withstand it for more than another minute or two.

After thirty minutes the pain has completely subsided and we feel at ease. Not to worry though, as this feeling will not last.

After forty minutes the pain has returned with a vengeance!

After fifty minutes we begin to feel blissful and praise ourselves for having gone through whatever it takes to cross over to the promised land!

"Such is your everyday mind," Sensei would say. "One moment you feel life couldn't be worse, and the next moment you can't even remember what your pain was all about. You make it all up, the good *and* the bad, and your experience has little if anything to do with reality.

"Indeed," he would say, "when you sit *seiza*, doesn't it become clear that the pain is in your head, and not in your legs? Or perhaps I should say, you manufacture the pain in your head with just a little bit of input from your legs.

"Why is it," Sensei would ask, "that no matter how hard you try, you can't make the pain go away? Yet at some point without any directions from 'you,' all of a sudden the pain is gone! Doesn't that make you feel a bit foolish?

"Tell the pain to go away, order it to go away, and it says 'No thank you.' But then at some point, and you never seem to know when or how, all of a sudden with a mind of its own the pain disappears. If you learned to control your thinking mind, then you would also learn to control your pain.

"The longer you study, the more I hope you'll realize 'reality' is a very slippery concept to grasp. The more you study the more you'll realize you don't understand what 'reality' is. Or perhaps it's better to say, you'll come to realize that reality is an illusion.

"You see, 'reality' and 'pain' are very much alike. Both are just figments of your imagination. Inventions of your thinking mind. Do you realize for instance, that when you look at and make sense out of something, 10% of the information comes from your eyes, and 90% of the information is made up inside your head. And that's not just my opinion, my reality; that's what research scientists say after many years of study.

"Part of the reason why I sometimes have you sit in *seiza* for long periods of time is that I want you to realize that your thinking mind is like an undisciplined child. The undisciplined child cries and cries for what he wants, and then once he realizes that he isn't going to get it, he finally shuts up and usually falls asleep soon after.

"When we sit in *seiza* I see most of you are crying out from inside yourself. Some of you actually give up, get up, and go home. But if you stay, at some point you realize you're not going to get what you want by crying. When you finally stop crying and accept what is, the pain you've manufactured inside your head goes away, and you get what you've been wanting after all! Such is life. Cry less, and try less, and you'll wind up suffering much less as well."

THE BENEFITS OF SUFFERING

One morning after a sitting meditation, Sensei looked around the class and began to speak.

"I'm always quite intrigued when I read about monks and priests from the West expressing the same sentiments we have here in Japan.

"I recently read that the Trappist monk Thomas Merton said, 'I became a monk not so as to suffer more, but to suffer more effectively.' Now I can't say that's what led me to study Aikido, but I can say the principle Merton Sensei expressed is one that has guided me over time.

"The more new students go on about how excited they are to be studying Aikido, the more I suspect they're trying to escape from suffering. They fail to realize that their misery is created by their beliefs and not by the outside world. Trying to run away from suffering is like trying to run away from yourself. Anywhere you go, anyplace you move to, you'll only find your negative beliefs waiting to welcome you as you arrive. And that's why in Aikido we look to create a tiny bit of suffering with some of our practices. It's a good way to see whether you are still trying to escape.

"You see, the way you respond to what's taking place says much more about your beliefs than you realize. Some of you have started to realize that your tendency is to try to escape from an attacker rather than joining with him. You'll never be able to escape the attacker, because you'll never be able to escape from yourself.

"I believe people increase their suffering each time they try to avoid it. In attempting to escape from your pain rather than settling into it, you set the stage for further misery. Some degree of pain is inherent to the human condition.

"If you've been coming to class for a while now, you've heard me ask this question before: 'If it wasn't for your suffering, who would you be today?'

"Your answer will say a lot about the way you feel about yourself, the manner in which you approach learning and change, and the reason you come to class. You will improve the quality of your life by immersing yourself in your struggle rather than looking to escape from it. By realizing that pain is something you create inside your head.

"I suggest you ask yourself, 'How does my perception of my current problem, my current struggle, mirror my overall beliefs in life?'

"If your current situation stayed the same but you changed your belief system, would you still be suffering? How would your problems appear to be different if you were different?

"Happiness and suffering are two sides of the same coin. Look for the happiness inherent in your current suffering, rather than looking to fix what you perceive to be wrong.

"When you are miserable, your emotional mind and your rational mind are locked in combat. Instead of fighting against yourself, use your whole self to stay cooperatively engaged in your struggle and you'll find that something within you shifts. Over time your struggle will be transformed into a life-affirming lesson.

"When you feel ill at ease in the world, it's a signal that part of you is calling out for help. When you willingly heed this call, the value of your struggle becomes apparent. I think we find no greater example of this than when a person is diagnosed with a life-threatening illness. Disease is the body's way of telling you that the way you're leading your life isn't working. Your symptoms are alerting you to the need for change. Be thankful for the feedback. Without it, you would soon no longer be alive."

CHAPTER 6

MU

ABOUT THE KANJI

MU (na) - THE VOID, NOTHING,
NON-EXISTENCE, TO REMOVE

*One of the concepts that has most fascinated me in Japan is **mushin**, which literally translates as 'no mind'.*

*Mushin is a peak performance state in which you discard all extraneous action and thought. In that state you are economical, ecological, and graceful, and you seek to follow the path of least resistance and optimal effect. **Mushin** is the experience you have prior to reflecting on what's occurring. In that state, you are dynamically relaxed, and have an open focus perspective. Because thought and action occur simultaneously, nothing comes between them, and nothing is left over or undone.*

MUSHIN

From time to time I get to meet exceptional teachers in Japan. Often what happens is that I go visit a friend, and it turns out that one of the other guests is a highly regarded *sensei*.

Recently I had the opportunity to meet a man by the name of Okamoto who works as an architect. Here is what Okamoto Sensei had to say about his work.

"Charlie-san, our host said you have an interest in architecture. She suggested I tell you about the concepts that influence my work, and so I've taken some time to think about this topic. In Japanese culture, and particularly in Japanese architecture, *mushin* is an important concept to understand. In relationship to my work, the two ideas I hold in regard to the meaning of *mushin* are "innocence" and "freedom from obstructive thinking." I strive to make all my work as simple as possible, without any visual, emotional, or physical obstructions.

"What I've found over the years is that the simpler you make something, the more obvious the obstructions in your thinking appear. Rather than being bothered or constrained by the relationship between simplicity and obstruction, I find it very energizing. In the early stages of each new design, I look forward to discovering the weakness in my thinking. This leads me to understand that I sometimes try to hide my weaknesses by obscuring them with complexity. The more simple the design, the less there is to hide behind. I must say that each time I discover this I am humbled. It's only by being willing to own up to my many personal flaws that I can little by little do away with the flaws in my designs.

"In both my personal and professional life, I attempt to discard all extraneous actions and thought. I strive to be economical, ecological, and graceful, and to follow a path of least resistance and optimal effect. I've found that I am most likely to embody this way of being prior to reflecting on what I'm doing. At such times, which still only happen rarely for me, I'm in a state of open, focused relaxation, and my thoughts and actions occur simultaneously. Nothing comes between my thoughts and my actions, and neither is anything left over or left undone. When I'm able to embody such a state I feel better both physically and emotionally, and I consider my work to be a reflection of my soul."

Sensei paused to make certain he still had my attention. "At the risk of filling the space with too many words," he said, "let me just say one more thing. The *Tao de Ching*, a classic Chinese text of wisdom, says the following:

> *Doors and windows are cut out from walls to form a room.*
> *It is the emptiness that the walls, floor, and ceiling encompass,*
> *that provides a space to live in.*
>
> *Thus, what we gain is Something, yet it is from the virtue*
> *of Nothing that this Something derives.*

"If you've ever been in a traditional Japanese room or Zen temple, you'll see that these spaces are filled with the same emptiness as described in this statement. Space is filled with nothing, as a way to allow for the infinite potential a room encompasses. This is an important part of the Japanese design aesthetic. The experience of emptiness is an invitation to empty one's thinking mind, so that a new, innocent reality might appear."

THE EBB AND FLOW OF LIFE

During my first year in Japan I hitchhiked for two weeks, visiting rural fishing villages on the west coast of Japan. At the time I spoke very little Japanese, and relied on the kindness of the people I met.

I visited tiny villages that had no hotels and rarely encountered tourists. Upon entering a village, I would find a kind-looking soul and pantomime that I needed a place to sleep. When my acting skills proved sufficient, I wound up in the house of a family willing to take in visitors for a small fee. After eating with my hosts, I would then be led to a simple room to sleep in.

In one village I had the privilege of staying with a remarkable man and his family. One night Ishida-san and I sat on a small wooden dock by the ocean. Using lots of gestures to help me understand, the man told me about his life. He was 63 years old. As a boy he'd been very involved in studying karate, but at the age of nineteen his life changed dramatically. Working on his father's fishing boat in rough seas, he lost his balance, and fell just as he was throwing a heavy fishing cage overboard. His left leg got caught in the line attached to the cage and the damage caused to the muscles and nerves of his left calf was severe. This left him with a permanent limp.

Once he realized he'd no longer be able to study karate, he made a firm commitment to use his life as a fisherman to further his studies. He read various books written by martial arts masters and then applied the principles of what he learned to his work life.

"One of the most important things I learned," he said, "is to create a rhythm with your posture, movements, and breathing, that matches the rhythm of nature. When I injured myself on the boat, I was so involved in handling the heavy cage that I lost touch with the flow of my surroundings. I was fighting against the ocean, rather than moving with it. Guess what? The ocean won!

"Notice the gentle ebb and flow of the ocean as we sit here now," he said, "and the sound of the tide lapping against the pilings of the pier.

 "As you sense the movement and sounds of the ocean, notice your breathing, and feel your body responding."

I began to do as he suggested and felt myself being drawn into a parallel world that was outside my everyday awareness.

"Feel the life force of the ocean, and without doing anything, allow yourself to move with the ocean.

"Breathe, move, and feel your heartbeat.

"Invite your heartbeat to synchronize with the heartbeat of the ocean.

"As you become one with the water, you might sense the fluids in your body ebbing and flowing, like the ocean entering into a shallow inlet filled with coral.

"Like the ocean, you can begin to feel the power of flowing without resisting. Flowing without fighting against anything.

"Water surrounds and moves past all obstacles, and you can do the same. Simply flow.

"A single drop of water, has no power. A single drop of water moving with the flow of the ocean forms a wave. The power of the wave comes from joining with. The same is true of me and you."

We sat there together for a while. The man, myself, and the ocean.

Not separate, but together.

In that moment I sensed all power comes from the same source.

EVERYDAY MIND AND YOUR CONCEPT OF TIME

"How unstable was your thinking mind?" Sensei asked, after we had just spent an hour doing a specific breathing exercise. "I'm guessing that in the last hour most of you were very busy thinking, even though you're meant to sit quietly when doing this exercise." When I heard him say this I wasn't sure whether to smile or frown, because he was certainly describing me!

"Such is your everyday mind." Sensei continued. "You don't know how to stop yourself from thinking, and the more you try to stop, the more thinking you do. Instead of experiencing the here and now, you run around in your thinking mind worrying and wondering about the past and the future. It's my guess, that many of you spend very little time living in, and enjoying the reality of the present.

"In fact," he added, "the more you study, the more you will realize you do not understand what reality is. You will come to realize that what you usually think of as reality is really only the content of your thinking mind.

"Rather than trying to understand reality, I think we can better spend our time exploring relativity. By exploring how each thing, each thought, each feeling, is relative to all the rest of your experience, you can learn a great deal. Relativity teaches us there is always more than one perspective, always more than one belief, always more than one understanding, in regard to any one moment in time.

"Einstein talked about placing his hand on a hot stove for one minute, and how that minute felt more like an hour. He then talked about sitting with a pretty girl for an hour, and how that hour seemed to pass so quickly.

"What he describes is very much like the experience of sitting and breathing. Minutes of chaotic thinking feel like hours, and calmness passes you by all too quickly. You manipulate and distort time, and you create a sense of connection with or separation from life itself.

"A human being is one infinitesimal part of an infinitely large universe. A tiny, tiny, something, existing for a few moments in space and time. When we feel separate from the rest of life our pain and suffering increases, as does our distortion of time. When we feel ourselves fully connected to life, everything is just as it should be.

"When I have you sit and breathe, I usually start by taking down the clock at the back of the *dojo* and placing it outside. You all see me do this. and yet many of you look back numerous times for the non-existent clock. With your sense of time so distorted, I wonder what information you're hoping the clock will provide." I felt embarrassed when I heard him say this, because more than once I was certain I could hear the clock ticking!

"Our belief in and dependence on time creates a kind of prison that restricts our ability to fully live and experience life. In the course of your study it's my hope that you'll begin to free yourself from this prison and experience how you share your pain, your pleasure, and indeed all of your life, with the rest of the universe. The more you can realize you're not alone, not separate, the more you'll realize just how fleeting every moment is. Both the pleasure and the pain. It's all to be experienced, appreciated, and then let go of, so that you can be ready for your next experience."

THE RELATIVITY OF EXPERIENCE

"Most everything I teach you," Sensei said, "is something I directly learned from someone else. Today, I would like to tell you a story one of my *sensei's* told me a long time ago."

Many years ago there was a young man living in a large city in Japan who felt his life was quite empty. In the hopes of attaining inner peace, he shaved his head and went to live in the mountains as a recluse.

After studying diligently for ten years, the man realized he still didn't understand how to live with a sense of emotional balance. Talking with other disciples, the young monk learned of a highly evolved Zen master living in China. He had a strong desire to study with this man and thus finally realize his true self.

He gathered his meager belongings, crossed the Sea of Japan, and started a long and arduous journey to the distant dwelling of the monk.

Every day he walked for many hours, stopping for the evening only after finding a patch of land that had a natural source of water safe for drinking. After traveling in this manner for more than a month, he had the strange sensation of feeling both energized and empty.

One day was particularly hot and dry, and the monk walked endlessly, unable to find water. As the day turned into a moonless night he finally came across a meadow. Totally exhausted, he collapsed onto the ground and began crawling around in the darkness in search of liquid sustenance. He came across a roughly made cup that had been left behind. The custom of leaving a cup with some water in it for the next traveler was quite common, so he drank the meager amount of water that remained. Drinking it with relish, he felt blessed and at peace with the world. He soon lay down and slept comfortably until awaking to the light of the early morning sun.

Upon sitting up, the first thing he noticed was what he had taken to be the roughly made cup from the night before. Indeed it was not a manmade cup, but rather the shattered skull of a baby wolf! The moist skull was caked with blood, and a number of ants were crawling around inside scavenging for food to carry back to their colony.

The monk saw all this and immediately began to vomit! He was overcome by several waves of nausea, and as the fluid poured forth from his mouth and nose, he clearly experienced his thinking mind overwhelming his body and his emotions. Unable to resist the repulsion his thinking had created, he understood that his thinking mind had been overwhelming him his entire life!

The night before the water had tasted delicious and he had felt refreshed. It was his misunderstanding of the circumstances that led him to feel fine. Upon seeing the skull and the ants in the light of the morning sun, it was his memory of his past actions and not the putrid water that brought about his nausea.

It was suddenly clear to him that—regardless of whether he was understanding or misunderstanding—it was his thinking mind that determined the way he felt. If his thinking was capable of creating suffering, it was also capable of creating peace of mind. What had occurred in the past was much less important than the way he reacted in the present. Upon understanding this, he realized his journey was complete, and he returned home to live his life with a sense of emotional fulfillment."

SEDIMENT

Back when I was a young student of Aikido, immediately after class was over, I would typically write down whatever Sensei had said that caught my attention. I rarely wrote down the finer points of a particular technique. Instead, I was drawn to the things Sensei said that related to something else, something not obviously pertaining to Aikido. After a while I created a notebook which I entitled "Sediment." Here's some of what I wrote in that notebook more than twenty-five years ago.

Health will follow sickness, and happy will follow sad. All life is cyclical. When you are able to keep this in mind you'll be a lot less concerned by the seemingly bad things that occur in your life. Good balances bad; life balances death.

It's important to believe in a truth that's bigger than the one you construct in your head. It's important to understand that life is not all about you.

You will never be able to believe in any person or thing more than you can believe in yourself. With goals and activities, if you believe you can't, you won't.

All of life is offering you energy and this energy can be converted into fuel for living. When you release all the muscles of your body and breathe freely, you're much better able to take in the energy that's available to you. This is the essence of high quality health. The more you hold on with the muscles of your body, the less oxygen you are able to take in. The less you're able to take in, the more you'll believe in scarcity.

To a large extent, your body is the product of your thinking. What you think about and what you believe in determines your health and what you get in life. Your thoughts have energy. When the energy within your system moves freely it sustains your life force. When the energy within your system is blocked or excessive your life force works against you. Worry less and you'll have more. Maintain a calm, clear focus and your life and work will flow freely.

Whatever you try to avoid or resist you tend to make stronger. That's how virulent forms of disease get going in hospitals. Whatever the antibiotic doesn't kill gets stronger. The more you talk and think about what you don't want, the more you starve what you do want. Your thinking mind creates a thought field. Your thought field is an energy field, much like an electrical grid. Your energy field attracts certain kinds of energy and people while repelling others. What and how you think determines who you become.

Your thinking mind determines the way you use your body and breathe. The way you use your body and breathe determines your emotional state and overall health.

Your body, just like the body of a classical guitar, is a resonator. When you adopt an open balanced posture, you increase your capacity to resonate and attract life sustaining energy.

The power that flows through you is limitless. The essence of who you are is not constrained by time, space, or your thinking mind. If you are truly emotionally healthy, you will tend to be physically healthy. The opposite of this is equally true. Your emotional health and your physical health are in a constant, recursive conversation.

You are the creator of your entire experience of life. This includes your health, your happiness, and your relationships ... or the lack thereof.

Your system is designed to be self-healing. Release all stressors and the body will heal itself. Stress is simply excess energy trapped in your body. This excess energy will search for a way to exit your system and be free. In an attempt to escape, it will attack your weakest link and begin to break it down. Let your energy be free, and it will work with you and for you.

CHAPTER 7

AIKIDO

ABOUT THE KANJI

*ai*KIDŌ - AIKIDO

The Japanese martial art of Aikido is made up of three kanji, which are read ai, KI, and DŌ. The first kanji ('ai') means "to combine, unite, join, or merge". The second kanji ('KI') means "spirit, life force, or energy". And the third kanji (DŌ) means "path, road, and method". This last kanji is often used in words connoting an artful path of study. Aikido offers students the opportunity to cultivate an enduring sense of cooperation, compassionate power, and respectful engagement with seeming adversaries. It is an art of peace-making.

LEARNING HOW TO LEARN

The more I absorbed the teaching of my Aikido *sensei*, Koichi Tohei, the more I realized I needed to adopt a different style of learning.

Tohei Sensei is charismatic and spontaneous when he teaches, and sometimes he would get a bit frustrated when students tried to write down his every word. Once he playfully said to a student, "Perhaps you should read my book before coming to class again. Then you won't need to take so many notes!" And guess what? The student actually wrote down those words!

"The reason for coming to class," Tohei Sensei would say, "is not to take notes. The reason for coming to class is to learn how to trust the intelligence of your body. In Aikido you have the opportunity to learn with your body while your thinking mind acts as a passive observer. Notice what happens at such times. Do you fall into a pit of internal dialogue and hesitancy, or do you perform with confidence?

"If you want to begin a process of transformation, you'll need to push past the barriers of your thinking mind. You'll need to have a sudden, and perhaps, unexpected experience, and then allow your learning to gestate over time. An understanding of what you learn with your sudden experience can only come later. Much later. So you'd better become comfortable with not knowing, and not understanding, while remaining confident that you are indeed learning.

"You see," he would sometimes say, "people rely too much on their rational mind, and don't believe they're learning unless they immediately comprehend what they've learned. I think you foreigners use the term 'He's in his head' to show that a person is absorbed in his thoughts and detached from the physical world.

"You, for instance." Tohei Sensei said while motioning towards one student. "You have been in Japan for a few months now, and you've

合氣道

learned the words for 'Good morning'. The problem is that you don't bow when you speak these words, so the meaning of your greeting is not received by others. I think this is because you were so busy writing down the words you didn't even notice the bowing. You were too busy being in your head. No matter what the topic, if you don't learn with your body as well as with your thinking mind, your learning will have little value.

"Many of you ask me over and over again to further explain what I've just said. I on the other hand, believe that additional explanations tend to lead toward additional confusion. You want to learn first with your head, and practice only after you've understood. This is exactly backwards from the learning process I'm suggesting. You need to trust that your body is indeed intelligent, and that you are indeed learning, even though your rational mind has yet to make sense out of what you're doing. All of the talking and notetaking you do winds up confusing you and makes your learning process more difficult than it needs to be.

"Learn with your body and then practice over and over again. Through practice you'll refine and come to understand what you've learned. Your Aikido practice is like what happens when writing a book. The author writes a first draft of a chapter, and then edits it nine times or more. That is one cycle of writing. In the *dojo*, you learn something new and then practice it ninety-nine times. This is one cycle of learning.

"There's a time for putting down your notes, and for most of you I'd say that time is right now. If you truly want to improve your ability to learn, you'll need to think less ... and do more."

PUNISHMENT AND THE CONCEPT OF 'RIGHT OR WRONG'

A lot of the best learning I received as an Aikido student came when we were outside of the *dojo* with Sensei. We could be having a cup of coffee or occasionally having a drink, and at some point it would become clear Sensei had a message to convey.

One day we were sitting in a coffee shop waiting for a train in the countryside. Seemingly out of nowhere, Sensei said, "I think there are many people in the world who act in a confrontational manner. I wish more people understood the Aikido principle of non-dissension.

"Instead of spending so much time and so many human lives quarreling over who is right and who is wrong, I think the world would be a better place if we spent more time exploring how both sides are both right *and* wrong."

I and the other two students sat there and said very little, knowing Sensei was just beginning to get warmed up.

"You see," Sensei said, "in Aikido we learn to refrain from engaging in confrontation. But that doesn't mean we shy away from protecting ourselves. It always intrigues me when new students attend a class and ask, 'How can Aikido really be a martial art if you don't attack or retaliate against your opponents?' By this time the three of you have heard my reply many times over. In Aikido we have no attack form because we have no desire or intention to harm our adversaries. Instead we strive to bring hostilities to a conclusion that is respectful of all involved.

"If my opponent has never harmed me, never struck me, never hurt me, then why would I want to hurt or punish him? Do I want to punish him simply because he has thought about hurting me, or because he has made a weak effort that was easily rebuffed? You see, even in a court of law, you can't charge someone with murder simply because they thought about murdering someone. Attempted murder and actual murder are two

合氣道

very different crimes. When I am relaxed, aware, and fully present in the moment, then my adversary will have little opportunity to successfully attack me. Since he hasn't hurt me, since he hasn't truly threatened me, I have little desire to punish him in any way. His own thoughts and the negative results he achieves in the world will be punishment enough.

"Related to punishing someone is the idea of someone or something being either 'right or wrong'. In Aikido, we learn to refrain from believing that one path or one way of thinking is inherently superior to another. We also learn to refrain from engaging in thinking that any one point of view is the opposite of another.

"When we think in terms of opposites and disagree with someone else's opinion, we begin to oppose the other person's point of view. And this is exactly the kind of thinking that leads to resisting, combat, antagonism, and an overall disrespect for our perceived adversary.

"In Aikido, we do not attack, but we also do not concede or give up. In every day life the same can be true. Without attacking the viewpoint of others, without conceding or giving up our own viewpoint, we can still maintain ourselves and continue to act in a way that is consistent with our beliefs.

"Keep that in mind," Sensei said as he looked across the table. "More than once I've heard you arguing with other students, trying to prove your viewpoint was more correct than theirs. When you act like that, not only will you fail to convince them that you are right and they are wrong, you'll also wind up losing them as friends and allies."

A CRISIS OF FAITH

People often ask what led me to begin studying Aikido. One of the first things that drew me was the understanding of how important our belief system is in regard to what kind of people and situations we attract. Here's what Sensei had to say in this regard.

"Many of you come to class not realizing that you are suffering from a crisis of faith. The less you recognize this, the more it winds up affecting everything you do.

"With some of you I get the feeling that you're sitting there, dreading what might go wrong, dreading that you might come off as incompetent or unconfident. When I look around to gauge how everyone's feeling on a given day, many of you look everywhere else but at me. It's as if you were saying, 'Please don't call on me Sensei!' And yet supposedly you're here to learn. What this tells me is that your body is in the *dojo*, but your thinking mind is somewhere else.

"Take stock of yourself now. Is your posture open and expansive? Are you breathing freely and easily? Is your muscle system relaxed and at ease? If not, you're almost certainly not feeling confident.

"What are your afraid of? The attack of your counterpart who is simply performing his half of a training task? The judgment of people watching who might say you're clumsy and unskilled? Or perhaps deep down, what you fear most is the attack of your own negative self-judgments, your lack of faith in yourself as a competent learner.

"What would your life be like if you believed you were a fine person, an intelligent person, and an overall good learner? What would your life be like if you didn't think something was wrong with you? If someone said you were a wonderful person, many of you would be quick to reply, 'Oh no, not me!' But if someone said you had a lot of problems that needed fixing, many of you would be quick to agree. I talk to you over and over

合氣道

again about the importance of being fully present in class. Just as you take off your slippers and leave them outside the *dojo*, you need to leave your limiting beliefs behind when you come to class. I know that isn't easy to do, but 'easy' isn't what is important here. Your aim should be to trust in yourself, and to notice when you go inside your head searching for negative memories every time you don't have immediate success.

"The principles of Aikido are actually rather simple, but simple does not mean easy. In fact, I have found that doing things simply usually takes lots of practice and hard work. That's partly because we tend to think too much and make things more complicated than they really are. If you start out lacking confidence you will expect difficulty. When you expect difficulty, it means your head is already filled with thoughts before you even begin. The more thoughts you have filling your head, the less you'll be able to notice what is, and the less you'll be able to perceive simplicity.

"Every accomplished artist, whether a ballerina or a boxer, performs with grace and ease. They can do this because they have pruned away everything that's not essential to their performance. They have snipped and trimmed until all of the complications and difficulties have been removed. With less to pay attention to they can give much more attention to what's left. Being confident in their ability, there's no separation between thinking and doing. There is only unity and integration.

"Take stock of yourself now. Is your posture open and expansive? Are you breathing freely and easily? Is your muscle system relaxed and at ease? If so, you will have have overcome your crisis of faith!"

THE MIND OF AIKIDO AND WATER

While in Japan I've had the opportunity of meeting many exceptional people. One of those was Senta Yamada, whom I met for the first time when visiting a friend.

Uncharacteristically for a Japanese person, Yamada Sensei moved his hands a lot as he spoke. He did this to portray his perception of the movements essential to what he called the 'mind' of Aikido and water, whose relationship he explained as follows.

> While you sit there, please breathe freely and move
> your body slightly, so that you can feel the movement
> and mind my words suggest to you.
>
> Water unites all the world's land masses, large and
> small, connecting what is seemingly separate, distant,
> and different into one seamless spherical whole.
>
> Water has an intelligence, a mind. In Aikido we strive
> to embody this same intelligence.
>
> We direct the flow of our energy so that it accords with
> that of others. When encountering those appearing
> angry and frightened, we make special effort to
> dissolve any sense of separation, distance, or difference.
>
> And even when moving away from others, we do
> so with the intent of joining with and returning
> back to them.
>
> Water not only joins together the land masses of earth,
> it also unites the earth and sky via never ending cycles
> of precipitation, movement, and evaporation.

合氣道

This is the same process human beings mirror in birth, life, and death.

Just like water, we come from heaven, spend time on earth, and return back to heaven once again.

Becoming, being, receding. Living, dying, recycling.

Water expands and contracts depending on the circumstances, and the same is true of the human spirit.

When you are harsh to a child, his or her spirit contracts.

When you love a child, his or her spirit expands.

The presence of water throughout our ecosystem is similar to the presence of fluids in the body, enveloping and uniting its cells and tissues.

The mind of water, the body's circulatory system, and Aikido, all have the same intention—to move with, absorb, nurture, cleanse, renew.

When everything is experienced as an integral part of the *One*, there is no disease, no attack, no separation, death, or destruction.

Regardless of the form it may take—rain, mist, steam, dew, snow, ice—water always has a spherical mind.

This mind of roundness is a key principle in the mind of non-dissension.

In Aikido we project a full round presence to our
adversary and flow with their movements.

Just like water, we offer no hard surfaces to bump
up against, and nothing to grab hold of.

We encourage our adversaries to follow their course
of action to its likely outcome, in the same way water
follows the path of gravity downhill ... ever moving
towards center until the time of renewal.

Regardless of the obstacles it encounters, water does not
stop, it does not give up.

It searches endlessly for the path of least resistance, and
when it meets resistance it rests, consolidating its power
until it is time to rise up again.

Waiting for another opportunity. Waiting for the
proper moment ... an opening.

A single drop of water has little power, but many drops
joined together can sweep away everything in their path,
with the relentless force of a tsunami.

Water joins with, is absorbed by, and surrounds.

It does not strive to act separately, but waits to be
moved by the forces of nature.

With a constant mind of effortless rest, renewal,
and movement.

As calm when doing as when simply being.

We can realize the end of every journey as a
new beginning, every destination as temporary,
every goal as cyclical.

合氣道

Beginning complete

We remain complete

With nowhere to go

Nothing to accomplish

Nothing to fulfill

Except our destiny.

Our returning

Is never in question.

WHAT HAVE YOU COME HERE TO LEARN?

When new students showed up in Aikido class, one of Sensei's favorite questions was, "What have you come here to learn?"

When Sensei asked such a question, you could be sure he wasn't going to accept the first answer someone gave. I was intrigued to see that no one seemed to have a reply that was well thought out. Myself included!

The longer I studied Aikido the more I felt Sensei's question was a kind of Zen *koan*, a paradoxical question designed to show the inadequacy of logical thinking. When he asked this question, a common scenario went like this:

"What are you here to learn?"
"I'm here to learn Aikido."
"Oh," Sensei would reply. "And what is Aikido?"
"Aikido is a martial art." the student would say.
"Ah, and what is a martial art?" Sensei would ask.
"A martial art teaches self-defense." the student would reply.
"Well, if your aim is to learn self defense, you could spend your time much more effectively studying Judo or Karate." Sensei would respond. "Perhaps you're in the wrong *dojo*."

I rarely raised my hand when Sensei asked questions, but once when he asked why we were sitting there in his *dojo*, I raised my hand and replied in a clear voice, "I don't know."

"Ah," Sensei said. "Finally someone with an honest answer!"

"If you don't know why you're here, why waste your time?" he asked.

"Well," I replied, "studying Aikido helps me understand that a lot of what I think I know doesn't hold up when put to the test. And a lot of what I do in life, I have no idea why I do it. Aikido is a mirror that helps me look at myself and realize my inadequacies as well as my strengths."

合氣道

Sensei smiled and said, "Not a bad answer. It's good to realize there is so much you don't know, as long as you are confident in your ability to learn.

"Everyone comes to class *wanting* something," Sensei said. "But few students come with the idea of giving. When you're filled with wanting, you feel empty inside and don't want to give away the little you have.

"A hungry man hoards what is his and doesn't share it with others. On the other hand, if you're already feeling full from all the knowledge you have, you won't have the hunger to learn something new."

Sensei pointed to a student who often came to class and said, "You tend to focus on wanting to perfect your technique, and you wind up losing sight of why you're here. If you were to focus instead on why you're here, your technique would likely suffer, and you would wind up with more questions than answers. Are you comfortable with not knowing?"

After a brief pause, he continued, "You need to pay attention while understanding that you won't know exactly *what* to pay attention to until after you've found it."

Sensei looked at another student and said, "When you stop fighting with yourself, you will realize you already have everything you need. Already having everything you need, you'll be much more willing to give to others. The more you give, the less there will be to defend.

"If you get to the point where you have nothing to defend, you'll discover no one wants to attack you. Once you've experienced this, your study of Aikido will take on a very different importance. Then you will be ready to take your learning to a new depth of self-discovery.

"You see," Sensei said, "the reason I ask these questions and say the things I do is that your reason for being here determines what you will learn and who you will become."

TAKE THE INITIATIVE BY DOING NOTHING

"You move so much that you're easy to hit and grab," Sensei called out to me. "You need to give your opponent a clearer target to strike at."

We were studying how to defend ourselves from multiple attackers. Five students rushed at me all at once, and once again I struggled to cope with them.

"OK, take a break," Sensei said.

"If all five attackers were able to hit you, then all five attackers would first need to reach you, is that not so?

"Your job is *not* to run away from your attackers so they can't hit you or grab you. Your job is to orchestrate everyone's movement, so all five attackers reach you at the same time. Think of the attackers as needing to pass through a gate. If they all try to rush through at the same time, they'll only wind up interfering with each other. Learn how to invite them in, and then open and close the gate in a way that is to your advantage."

Sensei had made similar remarks in the past, but accomplishing this in the heat of the moment requires a moving calmness that takes a while to get the hang of. You know in your head what you're *supposed* to do, but once your opponents are bearing down on you and your heart starts pounding, you find it hard to believe in what you've been taught.

"Think of it this way," Sensei said, as he pulled out a cloth he used to wipe away his sweat. "Here, take this cloth away from me."

As I grabbed for the cloth, he moved it closer towards me. Just as I was about to get a good hold on it, he let the cloth go and grabbed hold of my wrist. It didn't take but a split second for him to execute a painful wrist lock. The moment I started to feel the pain, I instinctively let go of the cloth, and he picked it back up with his free hand and placed it back inside his *dogi*.

合氣道

"You see," he said, as he let go of my wrist, "I'm not defending the cloth, I'm defending myself. Better to give you the cloth, because then I have both hands free to do as I need.

"When you try to escape, your opponents are in charge of the attack. When you move calmly and offer your opponents a clear target, *you* are in charge of the attack, and they rush forward to take advantage of the opportunity you've given them.

"When your thinking mind is calm, your body is also calm, and it is easy to understand what's happening. Your opponents will attack you in the same manner you reached for my cloth. They'll be confident about accomplishing their mission, because you've made it easy for them. The more confident they are, the less inhibition they'll have, and thus the stronger their attack. The stronger their attack, the more confused they will be when you take away the target at the last moment. During their confusion, you'll have all the time you need to do whatever is necessary.

"This is something that also often happens in your every day life," Sensei continued. "You feel like you are faced with a daunting task, and you make your task harder by moving about needlessly and losing your composure. Breathe deeply, be calm, and know the right moment will present itself if you have the faith to wait. Don't force the issue, and don't force the timing. Trust in the moment and trust in yourself. Take the initiative by doing nothing."

MOVE LESS, AND DO LESS, AND YOU'LL HAVE ALL THE TIME YOU NEED

In Aikido we have a special practice called "rondori," where you get attacked by several students simultaneously.

Now to be clear, none of your attackers are looking to do bodily harm. Mainly they're attempting to get ahold of you and take you down to the mat. When things don't go well you usually wind up getting caught from behind, wrestled to the ground, and subdued. When you're taking a nationwide test in front of a few hundred people, this can be a humiliating experience.

I was in a special class for advanced students and one of my Sensei's assistants was filming. The first time around, I was up against five very enthusiastic college students. I was quickly overwhelmed by them and Sensei was calling out to me, "Slow down, slow down!"

I felt like I was participating in the bull run in Pamplona and Sensei was suggesting I slow down so the bulls could catch up with me!

We tried the practice a second time. Sure enough I got trapped again, and once again Sensei called out: "Slow down!"

Shaking his head he asked, "Don't you believe me? The slower you go, the more in control you will feel. The slower you go, the sooner a path will appear. You need to be calm and pause, until an opening presents itself."

"Easier said than done!" I responded playfully.

"Of course it's not easy!" Sensei said. "If it were easy, it wouldn't be worth your time and effort. If you are looking for 'easy' you should study another martial art."

Having said this, Sensei got up and performed against the same five students. No worries. Everyone was quickly dispatched and Sensei was left standing on his own.

合氣道

Then, Sensei asked his assistant to show us the footage he'd been shooting. Sure enough, I looked like Charlie Chaplin trying to avoid oncoming traffic. Sensei on the other hand, seemed to be directing the traffic towards, and then away from himself.

Finally, Sensei asked his assistant to play the footage in slow motion.

"See," he said, "you are never calm, never still. You're trying to catch up with what's going on, rather than leading the proceedings.

"Notice the difference." he said, as we looked at the footage of him performing. "Movement, calmness, movement, calmness, and always in harmony with my breath.

"If I move too soon, they charge after me. If I pause just a moment, they rush to the spot where I *was*, and not to the spot where I am. They focus on the past, while I do my best to stay in the present.

"What's making this hard for you is your lack of confidence, and your belief that what you're doing is difficult. The more you hurry the more you worry, and the more your mind becomes scattered.

"A scattered mind has no focus, and no clear path. With no clear path, you become like a deer frozen in the headlights of an oncoming car. You become the prey.

"I don't want to overstate all of this." Sensei said, "But I'm guessing you might find the same to be true in your everyday life. Move less and do less, and the world will come to you. Move less, and do less, and you'll have all the time you need."

LIVING A SELF-FULFILLING PROPHECY

It was Friday night and the class was full. Over in the far right corner of the *dojo*, two students were giving each other a hard time, and I knew this was going to upset Sensei. Sure enough he growled at them a couple of times telling them to lighten up, but if anything they only became more aggressive. Finally Sensei had had enough and he called the class to a halt.

"Go to the front of the room," Sensei said to the two aggressive students. "I want you to perform for the class." Once they got there Sensei turned to the rest of us, gave a wink, and said "Now let's see which one of them is better than the other." He then told them to perform a specific sequence of moves.

Immediately, it looked like they were involved in a mud wrestling contest rather than Aikido. Both of them moved awkwardly, neither one of them had good footing, and it was hard to discern who was the attacker and who the defender.

After a couple minutes of watching, Sensei told them to stop and sit, as he moved to the front of the room. "There are so many things wrong here it's hard to know where to begin," he said. "The two of you perform as if you were identical twins. You look alike and have the same bad habits. I wouldn't be surprised if you told me you grew up in the same household.

"The first point that sticks out is that both of you act like righteous victims. Acting as if you're better or more correct than the one who is attacking you. With the mind of a victim, you are focused on getting attacked, rather than correctly focusing on nothing in particular. As I've tried to tell you many times before, you energize and strengthen whatever you focus on. So with your focus on the attack, you make the attacker stronger than he would normally be. Needless to say this leads to your self-fulfilling prophecy of performing poorly.

合氣道

"Next," Sensei said, "convinced you are not as good as you think you should be, you set about proving your various *dojo* partners are even worse. When attacking neither one of you attacks correctly. In fact, you both usually do the opposite of what you're supposed to do. When a specific technique calls for the attacker to overextend themselves by leaning forward, both of you under-extend and wind up leaning backwards. This makes the called for response to the attack more or less impossible to perform. You're not proving the incompetence of your partner, you're only proving how foolish you are.

"The last point I want to make for today is the following. It's amazing and sad to watch how strongly both of you critique each other, while at the same time neither one of you seems to have the ability to properly critique yourself. You each strive to increase your self-image by demonstrating how much more you know in comparison to your partner. You both have a strong desire to prove the other person wrong as a way of proving yourself right. This leads me to understand that both of you have little self-confidence and low self-esteem. Not only is neither one of you learning anything by practicing, you're instead strengthening the bad habits and lack of self-confidence you both had when first entering the *dojo*. I ask you now to bow and apologize to each other, bow and apologize to the entire class, and then please leave. Don't bother to come back again unless you're ready to change your mindset and cooperate."

MOVING FROM IDENTITY TO "WE-DENTITY"

The slippers each student wears from the changing room are meant to be neatly lined up at the *dojo* door. If necessary, you tidy up any slippers left askew. You do this because after a while it feels unsettling to see slippers out of place. You also do this because Sensei sends a student to make sure everyone and everything is ready before he makes his way to the *dojo*. Neatly lined up slippers is a way of saying, "We are ready to receive your lesson."

As Sensei enters the *dojo*, everyone bows to him while offering a greeting. When Sensei is ready to start the class, he takes his position at the front of the *dojo* and bows to us. Everyone is meant to bow in unison, but most often this doesn't happen to Sensei's liking. When the bowing rhythm of even one student is off, Sensei will bow again, requiring all the students to sense whether or not they are moving with the flow of the group. It's similar to playing in an orchestra. It's not acceptable to play your part as you wish. To do so would create noise, rather than music. Sensei is the conductor, and without any sheet music to read, you are meant to feel the flow and attune to Sensei and the group.

When the warm-up exercises begin, each student moves and calls out in unison, "One, two, three, four. One, two, three, four." Little by little we each begin to leave our separate identity behind. As everyone counts and breathes in the same rhythm, we start to experience a shift from identity to "we-dentity."

When he's in the mood to teach a bit of theory, Sensei might say, "People that breathe together tend to think and act alike. Group breathing leads to group mind and group mind leads you to understand that you're not alone, you're not separate. You share the oxygen in the room with everyone, and when you breathe together you send a wave of *ki* out into the universe. There is no better way to dissolve dissension than to breathe in harmony with your adversary. Sensing that you're both part of the same One, your adversary's fighting mind is less likely to manifest."

合氣道

At some point, with everyone standing, more complex movements are initiated. Specific placement of the feet and soft circular movements of the hips and arms are punctuated with a strong clear count.

"One, two, three, four. One, two, three, four." As the feet, hips, and arms move to the rhythm of the counting.

"One, two three four. One, two, three, four." Everyone moving together, counting together, and breathing together. Everyone shaping his or her individual activity to match and meld with the activity of others.

As the group's energy coalesces the mind of the group becomes One.

Movement, stillness, inhale, exhale. Movement, stillness, inhale, exhale.

"One, two, three, four. One, two, three, four."

Group action leads to "we-dentity" and a sense of compassion for those around you.

You sense that 'I' is much less powerful than 'We' ... You sense that 'I' is always embedded in 'We' ... You sense the power of individual minds melding into group mind. In the same way that countless drops of water join and move together to form a wave.

You realize attacking requires becoming separate ... Becoming separate, you lose the power of 'We' ... With no 'We' there is only 'I' ... When there is only 'I' you are no longer part of the wave. ...

And you exhaust and overwhelm yourself, fighting against the flow.

Life is here to offer you much more than survival. By joining in solidarity with others, we can create a world that is compassionate, collaborative, and plentiful.

CHAPTER 8

KOKORO

ABOUT THE KANJI

SHIN (kokoro) - HEART, MIND, SPIRIT, EMOTION

*The concept of **kokoro** has been a key factor in my fascination with various Japanese art forms. It has led me to understand that mind—and thus intelligence— are present in every cell of one's body. That if we are to be healthy and emotionally fulfilled, the thinking mind in our brain needs to work in harmony with the mind of sensation and relationship that resides in our body.*

FAKING IT

After I met my wife's *obaa-chan* a number of times, she stopped going to her hands and knees when bowing to me. Instead, she began to bow while standing.

The first time she remained standing, I worried that I might have done something to lessen her respect for me! Years later I realized she had begun to stand and bow as a way to show me that our relationship was becoming less formal and more friendly.

Having studied Aikido for a few years before first meeting *Obaa-chan*, I could see a definite similarity between the way she bowed to me and the way I was taught to bow to my *sensei*.

In Aikido class I was taught to first inhale and then begin my exhale and bow at the same time. When my exhale was complete, I was meant to pause for just a moment, and then finally rise up just as I started to inhale once again. This simple ritual, which involves integrating your breathing with your movement, can be very powerful. You feel a definite connection to the person you're bowing to, while at the same time feeling a deep connection to yourself.

Unbeknownst to *Obaa-chan*, I decided one day to playfully engage her in a bowing contest. My intention was to bow to her in the same manner as I bowed to my *sensei*. I was determined to bow deeper and longer than her in order to let her know that I felt *she* was the one deserving the most respect. I guess, in retrospect, I also wanted to show myself that my bowing was better than hers!

So I rang her bell and seized my chance.

She opened the door and bowed deeply as usual. Then, just as she bobbed up from her bow like a diver raising her head above water to get a fresh supply of oxygen, I began my bow. ... I stayed down as long as I thought

I could without seeming unnatural, and then just as I was coming up, I saw grandma going back down in the opposite direction, bowing even deeper than she had the first time, while once again mumbling wonderful things about me.

Not to be outdone, I waited patiently while pacing my breathing to her movements. Just as she started to bob up a second time, I began my exhale and went down a second time. I paused for what seemed like longer than I should have and then slowly came back up, only to see her going back down!

I'm not sure how many times we did this. Perhaps five complete rounds. All I know is that it seemed like an eternity.

It was as if we were connected by a system of weights and pulleys. Her coming up required me to go down, and vice versa.

From the first moment of my little contest, it was obvious to me that her bowing had a presence and a power that my bowing lacked. I felt like the guy you sometimes see in a photo that has an odd looking smile on his face: The smile is forced because he feels awkward but believes he needs to smile. The fact that I was only pretending to bow and show respect, and that she wasn't, was immediately apparent to me, and perhaps to *Obaa-chan* as well.

I was bowing with my body, but not with my heart. I wasn't bowing as an expression of my thanks. This left me feeling embarrassed, and I vowed to myself to authentically show her my respect in the future.

My little bowing contest taught me, that if the thanks and respect we show others is to have any real meaning, it must be initiated from a heartfelt sense of appreciation and humility.

ATONEMENT

I was out roller blading and exploring the side streets in my extended neighborhood, when I came across an older man and his granddaughter selling *origami* from their garage. They had some beautiful creations at very cheap prices, and I could see the young girl was anxious for me to buy something. So I spent a few hundred yen and was soon on my way, as I needed to get back home and prepare dinner.

A couple of weeks later I decided to see how they were doing, so I took a route that passed by their house. Recognizing me, the grandfather introduced himself as "Watanabe." When I inquired about his granddaughter, it turned out that she was at the dentist.

While taking a few minutes to get to know Watanabe-san, I noticed a poster that hung prominently on the wall. It told the story of a now famous Japanese girl by the name of Sadako Sasaki. Since my ability to read Japanese was limited, I asked him to explain what was written. Happy to oblige me, he recounted the following story.

"In 1945 Sadako Sasaki was at home when the atomic bomb was dropped one mile away from her house in Hiroshima. She managed to live another ten difficult years from that day, but eventually succumbed to leukemia, which she had developed as a result of her exposure to the nuclear fallout.

"While Sadako was in the hospital, her best friend came to visit, bringing with her an *origami* paper crane. Sadako didn't understand the meaning of the crane, so her friend explained—An ancient Japanese legend promises that anyone who folds a thousand *origami* cranes will be granted a wish— such as long life or recovery from illness or injury.

"Inspired by the legend Sadako worked tirelessly, making as many cranes as she could, but died shortly after finishing #644. Her friends completed the additional 356 cranes and buried them all with her.

"Over the past fifty years, the telling of this story has led to millions of paper cranes being made as a symbol for world peace."

As Watanabe-san finished talking I found myself tearing up. Someone had told me this story awhile ago, but at the time my Japanese was not good enough to grasp the entire meaning.

"You see," Watanabe-san said, "I started this *origami* project with my granddaughter for a number of reasons. I wanted to teach her the value of work, and that high-quality work can lead to a reasonable form of income. I also wanted to teach her the importance of paying attention to detail and turning out a first rate product. You need to be very exacting when making paper cranes ... otherwise you wind up with a mess. Lastly, I wanted to teach her about charity. She contributes fifteen percent of all she makes to the World Peace Foundation in Hiroshima."

Seeing that I was clearly moved by all that he had said, I had a sense Watanabe-san wanted to share something more.

"Sometimes," he said, "when no one has bought anything for a couple of days and my granddaughter is away, I place some money in the box and take out a few items. I give them to the nursery school down the block, and the little ones are always delighted to receive them. When my granddaughter returns I tell her someone came by and bought the cranes as a way of symbolizing their desire for world peace.

He grew quiet a moment, and this time it looked as if he were about to tear up. "There is one more thing," Watanabe-san added. "I served in the Imperial Army during World War II, and I am not proud of everything I did. I'm thankful that through my relationship with my granddaughter I've found a way to atone for my own past."

THE UNEXPECTED REWARDS OF EXITING MY COMFORT ZONE

I came to Japan twenty-five years ago with the express purpose of studying Aikido, as I had a vague goal of wanting to achieve some form of self-mastery. For my first three years in Tokyo I went to the *dojo* about thirty hours a week, which made it necessary for me to get up at 4:30 every morning but Sunday. Take a moment, put yourself in my futon, and imagine what it was like at times ...

It's pitch dark in the middle of winter, and the alarm clock goes off, interrupting my dream of lying on a warm beach in Bermuda. My hand ventures out from under my cozy covers to turn off what in my dream is a siren warning of a shark attack, and I suddenly realize there's no way it could be this cold in Bermuda!

The small kerosene heater in my room simply isn't able to keep pace with the frigid temperature, and in my internal dialogue I shout out, "Oh my goodness, I can see my breath!"

Somehow, miraculously, I did get out of bed every single morning. I must say, I often wondered what the drive was that led me to leave my "comfort zone" and venture out into the world.

Twenty-five years have passed since I first stepped off the plane, and I've known for a while that I benefitted greatly by getting up out of bed every morning. But the other day I learned in a very profound way just how important my years of training were. While out rollerblading I came towards a small intersection where I had the right of way. From the corner of my vision I saw a pick-up truck rocketing towards me from my right at about 45 miles an hour and still accelerating. He was very definitely on a collision path with me!

With no time to think, I instinctively began enacting what I'd learned in Aikido over the years.

"Blend *with* the attack," Sensei always said, and I did just that as I turned to my left to face in the same direction as the truck.

"Go with the attack," Sensei would call out relentlessly, and I did just that as I started skating in the same direction as the truck was moving.

"Perform with heart," Sensei used to whisper in our ear right before an important competition, and somehow I managed to do that.

As I turned to evade the truck, I moved just enough to avoid a direct hit. As the truck sideswiped me I let out a loud scream (in Aikido we call this a *ki-ai*), so I could give back to the truck all the energy it was sending my way.

The truck seriously grazed my left hip just as I hit the windshield with my left elbow. The explosive impact of my interaction with the truck threw me into the lower reaches of outer space, and thank goodness I had the knowledge stored in my body to do my very best Aikido roll.

As I laid on the ground dazed, I felt great exhilaration knowing I had made it through an event that could have killed me. As I lay there, I also slipped back twenty five years in time … feeling like I was once again lying on my futon on a cold winter morning in Tokyo.

From that place of past *and* present I knew two things for certain. One, was that my training will never leave me and never fail me. It's in my blood and in my soul. I have earned what I have learned.

The other thing I knew for sure was that no matter how difficult a situation might seem, I had the spirit to gather myself up with every ounce of courage I could muster, and face the challenges that lay ahead.

FEAR AND ANXIETY

From time to time, Sensei would talk to us about some of the mail he'd received from his students abroad. Here's what he had to say regarding a student's question about fear and anxiety.

"Recently a Belgian student sent me a letter asking about my thoughts on the high level of anxiety many people experience daily. In her letter, she said the word "anxiety" came from Latin, and meant 'a lasting state of fear.' Obviously fear and anxiety are important topics in the study of Aikido, but these conditions now also touch every level of society in most every country in the world. High levels of nearly constant fear and anxiety are leading to greater disease and increased societal problems as well.

"When you are anxious, you are fearful. When you are fearful, your heart rate and blood pressure rise, your breathing becomes shallow, your focus of attention narrows, and you generate high-frequency brain waves. All of which leads to the 'fight or flight' syndrome more and more people find themselves living in.

"In Aikido we see that 'fight or flight' winds up manifesting in the roles of 'attacker' and 'victim', and many people compulsively play out their parts as if on stage. It's important to note that the roles of attacker and victim are complementary in nature. Attackers need and search out victims, while compulsive victims need and search out attackers. I am sure you've seen this dynamic unfold in various family and professional relationships. Many of you come to class not realizing you're in 'fight or flight' mode. The less you recognize this the more you'll wind up compulsively acting out the roles of attacker or victim in class.

"Over the long term, fear and anxiety lead to a constant sense of emergency and a level of arousal that is unsustainable. On the one hand, if you are hyper alert, you'll wear out your system and wind up being unable to respond when necessary. On the other hand, constant warning signals generated by your unconscious mind lead you to eventually stop paying attention to the signals. Then, when a real need for action arrives, whether it's a virus or a belligerent person, your system will fail to respond in a timely manner.

"Take an inventory of yourself now. Is your posture open and expansive? If so, you will tend to feel ready to respond to life.

"Are you taking in lots of oxygen and releasing a complementary quantity of carbon dioxide? If so, you should be feeling at ease.

"Are your muscles relaxed and ready for action? Wild animals and high-performance athletes both know how to fully relax, right up to the moment of necessary action. How about you?

"Are you able to look out on the world with a soft focus gaze and open up to the world looking back at you? You can learn a lot by becoming aware of what and who you tend to avoid looking at.

"Can you hear the sound of a nearby ticking clock as you listen to a favorite piece of music? Is your heart warmed by the sound of a baby laughing? Are you comfortable with the sound of silence?

"When it's time to eat do you really taste and savor your food? When it's time to rest can you really let go?

"When you're sitting in the midst of your every day life, what's most real for you? Your many problems and fears, or the simple joy of being fully engaged in the here and now?

"Your emotional response to life depends on whether or not you are gently in control of yourself, engaged in heartfelt relationships, and in touch with your surroundings. Your emotional response to life is what determines your health and well-being. I hope you begin and end every day by smiling and saying 'Yes!'."

ON BEING A MAN

Wherever I am, drawing people into conversations that go beyond the surface is one of my favorite pastimes. I usually begin by sharing something personal about myself, while leaving the door open for others to do the same. In my Tokyo neighborhood I'm well known for this, and people seem to look forward to the opportunity of sharing time with me.

Recently I was sitting at the counter of a small Japanese restaurant talking to my long time friend Tabata-san. He is a few years older than me, and has always shown me a lot of kindness.

Somehow we got into talking about "being a man" and here is what Tabata-san had to say.

"Being a man in Japan is not easy. There are lots of expectations, and very little in the way of praise or reward.

"Boys in Japan receive a special status in their families because they're the ones who will carry the family name forward. This special status leads to special treatment, but also carries with it great responsibility.

"In particular, if you're the oldest son, traditionally this means you have the responsibility of living in your parents' house your entire life, and caring for them when they get older.

"Actually, if you get married, it will be your wife's job to care for your parents when they get older, but that's a story for another time.

"What happens for most Japanese boys is that early on they build a wall to hide behind. On the outside they act as if they do not feel fear, or even pain. But beneath the surface, a frightened boy remains.

"As boy-men, we wait our whole lives to be discovered by someone. We're hoping this someone will learn to read our feelings, because we're not good at expressing our feelings verbally.

"With me for instance, I'd like to be able to say 'I love you,' but I have never done so. To speak those words would simply be too much.

"Men don't feel the need to complicate things by trying to express in words everything they feel. But women on the other hand, and especially our wives, often ask us to talk about our feelings, and that makes relationships more complicated than they need to be. It winds up creating a distance between us that over time leads us to drift further and further apart. This sometimes leaves me feeling somewhat lonely, but I'm not at all sure there's a better alternative.

"Men want to be loved, but without the need to create further responsibility, as we already feel overburdened by the responsibilities our families and our companies place on us.

"Japanese men are so simple. Just like me! And in my mind, simple is better. But somehow, we often get asked to be more sophisticated, more adept at expressing the feelings we have been taught to hide.

"You know, just like me, my wife likes to have a drink from time to time. But you'll never see me out drinking with her, because she'll be sure to try and draw me into conversations that I don't want to have.

"She has her friends and I have mine, and I think in the long run keeping this distance between us is better, because it makes it easier to live together, rather than following the path of high expectations and high rates of divorce, like you have in the U.S.

"By the way," Tabata-san said, "you're beginning to look too serious. Why don't we talk about something else!"

THE THREE HEARTS OF A JAPANESE MAN

Well it's Friday night and I'm pretty certain my friend Tabata-san will be hanging out at the usual place. So I decide to go have a talk with him.

Sure enough, I find him sitting with a couple of young men telling them what Judo used to be like in the old days.

I wait patiently for an opening in the conversation, as I want to ask Tabata-san to talk more about something we'd discussed earlier—his experience of being a Japanese man.

Before I have the opportunity to ask, Tabata-san reads my mind and starts telling the two young men what he and I had discussed the last time out. Soon, the conversation segues into him talking about 'the three hearts of a Japanese man'.

"You see," he explains, "being a Japanese man is not a simple matter, even though life would be more enjoyable if it were. In order to make my way in the world, I myself, and I believe most Japanese men my age, find it necessary to maintain and nourish three hearts instead of just one.

"The first and most important heart I have is my private heart. The feelings I hold in this heart I don't share with anyone. With the exception being when I've had one too many beers." he says with a broad smile suddenly appearing on his face.

"I rarely share my true feelings with anyone, because to do so would only tend to cause complications and misunderstandings. This is a fact of life most every Japanese man comes to realize and live with over time.

"My second heart," Tabata-san says after a brief pause, "is my business heart. This is the heart that makes it possible for me to earn a living and make my way in the world.

"At work, you soon realize your superiors aren't interested in hearing what you hold in this heart. When your boss asks you, 'What do you think of this idea?', what's most important is that you spare him the embarrassment of being wrong. So you almost always say, 'Oh wow, what a great idea!'. If you are really clever, you will be able to correct the weaknesses in his strategy while having him think he came up with the changes himself.

"Freedom of speech, as it is guaranteed in the American constitution, is only granted in Japanese business circles after consuming a few beers. Drinking gives you the opportunity to share some of what you have been hiding. Everyone understands that whatever you say to your boss while drinking, is forgiven and forgotten the next day. Or at least that is the way it is in the company I have worked in for the last thirty-eight years."

Tabata-san pauses to see if we are still interested, and when I nod my head enthusiastically, he continues.

"Finally, I am left with my family heart, and I attend to this heart only after taking care of the other two.

"With my family heart I speak the words, bear the responsibilities, and perform the tasks every good husband and father is meant to. What is most important in this regard is maintaining the spirit of support and hard work that will lead to my children doing well in the world. I'm usually too busy and tired to do all that much with my family, but that is rarely a problem because I have my wife to tell me what to do and say, and when.

"Well, there you have it," Tabata-san says. "Charlie-san, you have invited me to explore the rewards of sharing my private heart, and I must say I'm still concerned about being misunderstood, or ridiculed. But you're right, it's quite fantastic to discover that most of the people around me have the same hopes and fears as me!"

CHAPTER 9

PURITY OF HEART

ABOUT THE KANJI

JI (itsuku) - PITY, COMPASSION, LOVE

*The spirit of **itsukushimi** is a wonderful caring
presence displayed by many of the fine women
I have had the honor of meeting in Japan.*

A WINDOW ON THE WORLD

'People watching' has always been one of my favorite activities, and there is no better place to do this than in a foreign culture. I've been in Japan for more than twenty-five years now, and in many ways I still feel like a stranger in a strange land. I say this in a totally positive sense, as I love being drawn into human interactions that leave me contemplating the richness of life.

One of my favorite rituals is breakfast in a local restaurant. I like sitting by the window, as the view gives me a wonderful perspective on the world. By observing the people outside without myself being seen, I get to take in life in a pristine form.

Some of what I get to see ...

People lining up for the seven o'clock bus every morning ...

What intrigues me the most is how the scene is almost always the same. The first person waiting is an elderly lady who invariably shows up ten minutes early. The last person in line is always a young guy who almost always trots to the stop thirty seconds before the bus is due to depart. It seems that he rarely allots enough time to getting dressed, as he almost always shows up with his tie in his hand. When the bus is late, he puts on his tie while waiting. If the bus has still yet to arrive, he usually pulls a wrapped rice ball out of his pocket and eats his breakfast. What a time-efficient way to live one's life!

A couple walking their dog together ...

I assume the couple is married. The husband walks the dog on a leash with his wife following about five feet behind. She carries implements for cleaning up after the dog. The husband talks to the wife without looking back towards her, and he's always smoking a cigarette. When he is done with his cigarette he lets his wife know, and she hands him a container. In goes the butt, and without missing a step he hands the container back to her. I am left wondering if they have any children, and what the nature of their overall relationship is like.

An elderly maintenance lady for the apartment building across the street ...

It is touching to see the dedication this woman shows in doing a job many would consider menial. Stooped over her short broom, she uses it as if it were a surgical instrument, taking care to clean the sidewalk of anything that might detract from the standard of cleanliness she has set for herself.

I have purposely walked past her building before she has come out, to get a sense of what she looks for when sweeping. Even though I often don't notice anything being amiss, this doesn't alter her routine one iota. Over the years, she must have developed a way of looking that is much more refined than mine!

I take in all these scenes from my 'window on the world' feeling cozy and safe, and then occasionally I realize I'm looking with my heart as well as with my eyes.

Recently, the cleaning lady did not show up two mornings in a row. I was concerned that something must be wrong, and on the third day I saw people placing flowers at a makeshift altar. When I asked one of the waitresses, she said the lady had suddenly passed away. I was touched to hear this, and purchased some flowers to add to the others already there.

I can only hope this special lady realized what a wonderful service she had provided for the entire neighborhood. Whoever takes over her job will have to work hard to maintain her standard of excellence.

Looking around me today, somehow the whole world seems a little bit less orderly.

A NEWFOUND FRIEND

Recently, as I was about to enter my local supermarket, I noticed a woman who was perhaps in her seventies, having trouble getting her left shoe back onto her foot.

The problem was that she couldn't find a good place to steady herself so she could bend over and adjust the shoe.

Without a moments thought, I came up next to her, kneeled down, and asked, "Would you like some help with that?"

"Oh, please!" she said. "I took my shoe off because it had a small stone inside, and now I can't get it back on."

I suggested she place her left hand on my shoulder. Taking hold of the shoe, I had her slide her foot in. It took just a moment and the task was done.

I motioned for her to enter the store before me, and she asked, "Is it OK if I go shopping with you?"

I wasn't sure what she had in mind, but I quickly said, "Sure, please join me."

The lady introduced herself as Okada. I told her my name was Charlie, and soon we were on our way, slowly moving through the aisles.

We hadn't walked but a few feet when Okada-san said to me, "I don't get to meet many foreigners, and you seem so nice. If you don't mind, I would like to buy whatever you buy. It would be like getting to eat a meal in a foreign country, only without the need to travel. Would that be OK with you?"

Her proposal caught me off guard and amused me at the same time. "Well sure!" I said. "I hope I buy things you won't mind eating."

Foregoing my initial reason for shopping, I quickly decided to buy food that would go together as a nice meal.

Some freshly cut basil, a head of garlic, a small bottle of olive oil (even though I already had some at home), a package of spaghetti, some gorgonzola cheese, a jar of olives, and a loaf of French bread. As I selected each item, I suggested what she could do to prepare and serve a well-constructed meal.

To top it all off, and as a way of seeing just how playful Okada-san was, I put a bottle of Chianti in my cart.

"Oh," she said, "is that wine?"

"Yes" I said, "It is wine. But there's no need for you to buy any."

"Do I have to drink the whole bottle at one go?" she asked.

"Oh no!" I replied. "That would likely be way too much for you. You can have a glass and save the rest for later."

"OK, then." she said. "I'll buy a bottle."

"I'm 80 years old and I married very young," she continued. "The only time I ever tasted alcohol was when I was serving my husband and his guests. I would sometimes take a sip or two in the kitchen to see what it tasted like. But then ten years ago when my husband passed away, I started to have a glass of beer once a week with dinner. After so many years of hard work it's wonderful to treat myself to such a luxury. I set the table with my best silverware and a cloth napkin, and then I sit down making believe I am in a fine restaurant. This will be my first time ever trying wine, and I'm going to make believe I am in Italy. Maybe I will buy a phrase book so I know what to say to the waiter!"

As she smiled warmly I thought to myself, "Isn't it wonderful to make friends with a lady that has such a wonderful imagination!"

ONE THING LEADS TO THE NEXT

Well, it was about a month since I had last seen Okada-san when I saw her coming out of the dry cleaners.

"How was your meal?" I asked.

"Fantastic!" she said. "In fact, it has led to a whole new life for me."

"Oh wow! Do tell me." I replied.

"Well," she said, "as you can guess, my house smelled of garlic the day after I made the meal you taught me how to cook. My friend Ishida-san came over to gossip, and she asked me why the smell of garlic was so strong. When I told her about the meal I had made, she asked if I would please invite her the next time.

"So, invite her I did, and we went food shopping together the following week. Ishida-san suggested we try the local sake shop for a better bottle of wine, and I agreed. While asking the sake master what wine he would suggest, his father came out from the back of the store. The father quickly proceeded to say that if we were kind enough to invite him for dinner, he would gladly bring the wine.

"Well, before I could think of how to reply, Ishida-san was bowing and nodding her head as a way of saying yes.

"Since then, the three of us have had dinner twice, and I must say I'm particularly glad to see you today because I'm in dire need of some new recipes!"

I told Okada-san I was unable to go shopping at the moment, but would be glad to meet her at 4 p.m. the following day. She quickly agreed.

Upon meeting, I asked her if she might like to learn how to make small pizzas, and needless to say she was enthusiastic about the idea of trying.

While we were waiting at the checkout line, Okada-san said to me in a fairly low voice, "There is something I did not tell you yesterday."

"Oh?" I said, giving her the chance to continue.

"Shimizu-san from the sake shop has expressed his interest in me. He has already sent me flowers once, and asked me to attend a *bonsai* exhibit with him."

"How nice!" I replied.

"Well, in regard to his invitation," she said, "I told him 'No.', and that a woman my age was too old to start dating."

"Oh," I said, not sure where the story was leading.

"He replied by saying a woman my age was just the right age for him. And I must say, he has gotten ever bolder since then."

"Oh my goodness!" I said jokingly. "Is there any chance we'll be hearing wedding bells any time soon?"

"Well," she said, "believe it or not, he has broached the subject as an alternative to dating!

"After recovering from the shock of his proposal, I told him I had no intention of ever doing the washing, ironing, cooking, and cleaning for another man. But he then told me that he had been cooking for the last eight years ever since his wife died, and even his son had said his cooking was good. And as far as the household tasks go, he said he'd be willing to learn if I would teach him.

"Since I wasn't about to say 'Yes', I didn't know what else to say to dissuade him. I wound up blurting out that if he was as awkward at doing that 'other thing' as my first husband, I would want the right to say 'No thank you'—a right I never felt I had before.

"His reply? That I could teach him about that after teaching him how to do the household tasks. So, I must say, he has left me feeling rather unsettled.

"Whether or not anything further comes from all this, I want to thank you in advance, because none of this would have been possible without you!"

"In that case," I replied with a deep smile in my heart, "next time I'd better think twice before removing a stone from someone's shoe!"

LOVE AND MARRIAGE

I saw Okada-san again yesterday and she got very excited when I told her I had written some heartwarming stories about her recently. Her face really lit up when I told her my stories were mainly read by *gaijin*.

"Oh my goodness!" she said. "Who would have ever thought I'd be playing some role in communicating to thousands of foreigners! I feel a bit like the foreign minister," she continued, "only without all the political responsibilities.

"Please be sure to tell everyone I said hello, and be sure to let them know that I bowed to each and every one of them," she went on, bobbing up and down all the while.

"You know," she said, "I can always tell whether or not people bow to me when hanging up the phone. Salesmen rarely bow, and some people who I thought would, don't. I find this rather disappointing. It's a shame people don't have more respect for each other.

"What will you write about next?" she asked, with the smile coming back to her face.

I knew that what she was really asking was, "What will you write about *me* next?"

"Well, I was thinking that perhaps you would tell me a story or two about your life, and I would relate your stories to my readers."

"Hmm," she mused, "that will take more than one cup of tea, won't it. Or perhaps you would prefer coffee. Why don't we go to the coffee shop that plays those old jazz recordings?"

So off we went, and here is the first story she had to tell.

"As you know, when I was a child almost all marriages were arranged.

When I was 21 years old, I came home from my job and was told by my mother that a good husband had been found for me. I wasn't surprised to hear her say this, but I also was not happy to hear these words. I had already been wondering for some time why it was assumed that I would have no real choice in the matter.

"My mom showed me a high school graduation picture of my potential husband. I remember thinking he looked way too serious. As it turned out, my first impression was rather correct.

"I was told that my parents and the boy's parents were just beginning to engage in talks, and that I would meet the young man only after my parents had decided everything was right.

"As it turns out, the first time I met Jiro was the day my parents said we were all meeting that evening to decide on the details of the wedding and reception. I just wasn't ready to hear these words and I felt quite shocked and lonely.

"We all met, and it was hard to know who felt more ill at ease, me or Jiro. I remember doing my best to smile as I said "Yes" whenever my opinion was asked.

"We were married several months later.

"On our way to our honeymoon my husband carried our two suitcases and was careful to hold doors open for me and let me go first.

"On the way home, I carried both the suitcases, and my husband walked ahead of me, never bothering to hold the door.

"What else can I say? Most of my marriage was conducted in the very same fashion. Such was often the case for young Japanese women in my day."

KANAI

I saw Okada-san on the street yesterday, and she invited me for lunch the next day at my favorite afternoon restaurant. She offered to treat me as a gesture of thanks 'for all my kindness'. I gladly accepted, and continued on my way to the train station.

When I arrived the next day, Okada-san was already there, and she had brought along Ishida-san, the women she had been trying my recipes with. I was touched to see them—with their radiant eyes and big smiles, they looked like two of Japan's national treasures!

Soon after we had ordered our meals, Ishida-san asked about the writing I was doing. She wondered out loud if perhaps she might have something 'small' to contribute. She obviously had some stories she wanted to share, and I must say, once she got going she had some powerful experiences and insights!

"Okada-san told me she talked to you some about her marriage," began Ishida-san. "Her marriage was perhaps better than mine, and I'd like to tell you a little bit about my own experience.

"Being married taught me a lot about myself, and a lot about Japanese culture," she said. "You might think it strange that I say I learned about Japanese culture, but being a young girl and watching my mom did not prepare me for what I eventually went through.

"As you probably know," she said, "when talking to others, a Japanese man refers to his wife as '*kanai*,' which literally means 'inside the house'. Nothing more. If you could read kanji but did not happen to know what this term meant, you might never guess it refers to a woman, or even a human being, for that matter.

"The wife on the other hand, when talking to others, refers to her husband as '*shujin*' which means 'master' or 'the person in charge'.

"I must say, to this very day I wonder why this is so. Are we meant to understand there's something inferior about women, or that men are just somehow more important? Frankly, I think this is one aspect of Japanese culture that could stand further scrutiny.

"From my husband's point of view, I feel I was meant to make life convenient for him. While for me, I felt left on my own and abandoned. I lived in the same house as him, and did everything I could to serve him, but at the same time we lived separately. He came and went as he pleased, and I was meant to always be prepared to serve him when he did come home.

"One of the strangest experiences life can offer a Japanese woman is the cycle of life involved with being a mother.

"I use the term 'strange' because most wives have sex with their master, even though they have very little in the way of a truly personal relationship with their master. In my marriage, the only time we had sex is after my husband had done a good deal of drinking and smoking. He smelled terrible, and I used to literally hold my breath, hoping he would finish as quickly as possible.

"But the strange beauty of all this is that I got pregnant three times, and raised three wonderful children that I was, and still am, very close to.

"So, out of a relationship that had a complete lack of intimacy and sharing, came three relationships that offered me deep levels of intimacy and sharing. Strange, isn't it?" she said.

"I'm sorry to have gone on for so long. Let's finish eating and talk about something more pleasant. Perhaps Okada-san has some new pictures of her great-grandchildren!"

PAMPERING MYSELF

As my relationship with Okada-san and Ishida-san progressed, I began to have lunch with them once or twice a month. Usually we would go to the same restaurant and spend at least an hour together. The more I got to know them, the more I was touched by their emotional honesty.

On one of these occasions, upon walking into the restaurant I could immediately tell that Ishida-san had something she wanted to talk about. No sooner had I sat down than she blurted out, "I have something I've been wanting to say for a long time." With a twinkle in her eyes, Ishida-san began, "I don't really know anything about the Catholic religion, but I think this must be what Catholics feel when they go to confession and talk to a priest."

I smiled, urging her to continue.

"Charlie-san, as I told you before, when my kids were still at home I used to sit around late at night, waiting for my husband to return. But once my kids moved out I got quite bored with all the waiting and more than a little resentful that my husband was out having a good time while I sat around feeling lonely and abandoned.

"One day when cleaning out the pockets of my husband's suit jacket before taking it to the cleaners, I found the business card of a famous restaurant in the Ginza district. I got a bit jealous and angry upon seeing this. I didn't want to sit at home by myself while my husband went to expensive restaurants.

"I knew business people took their clients to such places as a way to show their gratitude. But at home my husband was never grateful for anything I did. Indeed the only time he seemed to really notice me was when something was not to his liking.

"Somewhat impulsively, I decided I would go on my own to the restaurant shown on the business card. I wanted to find out what I had been missing. I figured if my husband had been there recently, he wasn't likely to go there a second time anytime soon. So off I went, not giving myself a chance to change my mind.

"The restaurant held about twenty tables, and around fifteen of the tables were occupied by older men in the company of much younger women. Upon seeing this I immediately sensed this was the kind of entertainment my husband was enjoying from time to time. Indeed when I walked in, being already in my fifties and by myself, the waiter seemed quite surprised when I told him I would be dining alone.

"I asked the waiter to help me order, and I decided to have the best of everything. 'Why not?' I thought to myself. If no one else is going to pamper me, I'd better get used to pampering myself. I must say I found the prices a bit overwhelming, but I made believe the bill was a business expense incurred by my husband. Needless to say, I paid in cash!

"And thus, my little ritual began. I would carefully check my husband's pockets and his credit card bills, and then once a month I would go to the very same places he went to. I must say I had a great sense of being naughty and subversive, and I found the whole experience quite delightful!

"Beyond fancy restaurants, I had one other place I would go to when I wanted to be pampered. The beauty salon.

"The women working there were kind and attentive, and they always complimented me on my appearance. They did this with all their customers, so I knew they weren't telling the truth. But it still made me feel good. Having someone treat me as if I were special is a feeling I've never grown tired of!

"One aspect of the beauty salon experience has always been quite obvious to me. The more expensive the salon, the more they pamper you. So whenever I was feeling particularly down, I didn't hesitate to go to a more expensive salon.

"Such is the life of many Japanese wives. If you want to be pampered from time to time, you may need to create the experience for yourself."

LOVE AND MARRIAGE, REVISITED

I saw Okada-san again today. It turns out that after my talk with Ishida-san, another friend has said she would also like to meet me. It seems that Okada-san has elevated our time together to the realm of 'interviews' and her friend Shimoda-san wants to tell her story. So I agree to meet the both of them the next day.

I arrive at our favorite coffee shop to find the two ladies already there. Okada-san handles the introductions, telling her friend I'm kind and gentle, and that she should feel free to speak her mind. Shimoda-san bows profusely as she apologizes for taking up my time. Announcing that she is 85 years old, she wonders aloud whether I really want to hear from such an elderly woman. When I tell her that at 62 I'm not so young myself, she places her hand over her mouth in shyness, and tells me that I am three years younger than her oldest child.

"Like Okada-san," she says, "the first time I met my husband to be was when both families got together to discuss the details of the wedding reception. Not only was my opinion not asked for, but they spoke as if I wasn't even in the room. I was just 19 years old, and young girls weren't meant to have opinions—even if the topic at hand was their upcoming marriage. My mother had already told me that she and my father had picked a suitable husband for me, and that I should not be egotistical, as my marriage would benefit both families.

"I have no idea what my mother meant with such words." Shimoda-san said. "I say this because still to this day, I feel that I was given over to my husband's family more as a slave than as a wife. And my parents didn't even receive any payment in return!

"Excuse me if I sound bitter." Shimoda-san continued. "I don't want to appear selfish or negative, but it's important that you understand my circumstances. I was 19 when I married and my husband was 24. He was already an alcoholic, and as the oldest son in his family, he was used to always getting his own way.

"Beyond my husband's bad habits, his family owned a restaurant in a very busy tourist area, and the restaurant was open 360 days a year. This was the life I was thrust into. Working seven days a week, fifty one weeks of the year, and having a five day vacation once a year in August.

"If that isn't slavery," she said, "then please tell me what is. I worked for the family business a minimum of twelve hours a day, seven days a week, while bearing and raising four children. I don't have the words to describe how challenging my life was. Being on my feet for hours and hours every day, while being pregnant and sometimes carrying my youngest child on my back. There's nothing worse than being eight months pregnant in August in Tokyo, on a 90-degree day with 90 percent humidity.

"Maybe the worst part of it was," Shimoda-san said as she wiped some moisture from her eyes, "that neither my husband nor anyone in his family appeared to care. Everyone just seemed to assume I would do whatever was necessary, with no regard for my pain and suffering. With no regard for my feelings.

"My husband passed away twenty years ago from cirrhosis of the liver. Since then I've been making donations to various organizations working to help women in third world countries. In this way, I hope my suffering has not been in vain."

THE POWER OF CULTURE

I ran some errands after my meeting with my two lady friends, and by the time I got home Okada-san had already left a phone message. She said Shimoda-san was feeling unsettled and wanted to further explain some of what she had said. Okada-san suggested it might be a good idea to meet at her house for dinner the following evening so that the three of us could talk at length.

When I arrived at Okada-san's house, she greeted me with a look that made me feel like a door to door salesman. Her face held little sign of her feelings, and the usual twinkle was gone from her eyes. I stepped in and saw Shimoda-san sitting in *seiza* by the low dining room table. She bowed deeply several times while expressing her thanks for my finding the time to come. She had a mask of worry and sorrow on her face, and I felt sad to see her looking so dark.

As I sat down at the table I playfully said, "I'm guessing our conversation will take more than one cup of tea to complete. What's on the menu?"

Thankfully, Okada-san took my lead and replied, "Well, being that it's evening and so hot outside, wouldn't we do better with a small glass of chilled sake?"

After the sake was served and we had lifted our glasses to a chorus of "*Campai!*", Shimoda-san began to share what was on her mind.

"I started to feel a lot of shame and guilt after our conversation," she said. "At first I thought it was because I'd spoken unkind words about the people I lived and worked with for so many years. In this regard I felt like a traitor. As if I had literally exposed their dirty laundry in public.

"But soon," she continued, "I began to realize I was mostly upset because of what I had taught my children.

"You see, just like my mother, and my husband's mother, I taught my children that the role of women was to serve men.

"I didn't want to be teaching them this, and I wasn't even aware until yesterday that I had been teaching them this. But after reflecting on our conversation I realized I had taught my children the very principles I was claiming to be so strongly against.

"I had two boys and two girls, and I explicitly taught my daughters to serve their brothers and bring them tea and snacks when they asked. But I never taught the boys to do anything at all for their sisters. Except, perhaps, for urging them to not be so harsh when their sisters were slow to serve them!

"Today I purposefully went over to the house of one of my daughters. While I was there I got my grandson to serve his younger sister and myself some snacks. I could see my daughter in the next room, and she looked somewhat surprised.

"When the children went out to play I called my daughter over and we had a wonderful heartfelt conversation. I apologized for not always being the best teacher or the best mother, and we had a bit of a cry and a good laugh as well.

"Even now, I'm sitting here wondering how in the world I could have taught my children something I don't believe in. It's all quite mysterious how I, as a woman, taught my children that women should subjugate their lives to men. I never before realized what a strong hold my culture has on my soul."

ABOUT THE AUTHOR

CHARLIE BADENHOP

If I had to use just one word to describe myself and my background, it would be *eclectic*. My life and my work have evolved through studying with many fine teachers from around the world. I am a native New Yorker, and in 1985 I moved to Japan to study Aikido, and *Noguchi Sei Tai*. I've been living here ever since!

My Japanese clients say, "Charlie-san has a foreign face and name, but a Japanese heart." My Western clients tell me I offer an intriguing Eastern sensibility, couched in modern terms. I'm glad to hear people say these things, because I love the combination and cross-pollination of Eastern and Western cultures that my work offers.

I am the originator of Seishindo. A human potential discipline that inspires people to live the life their true heart desires. The foundation of Seishindo derives from the theories of NLP, Ericksonian Hypnosis, Self-relations Psychotherapy, Aikido, and *Noguchi Sei Tai*.

In my work I strive to create a context in which people feel empowered to achieve their life's dreams. What's important to know in this regard is, you already possess all the necessary resources, to live the life you have been yearning for!

WOULD YOU LIKE TO TRAVEL WITH ME A BIT FURTHER?

I hope you have enjoyed exploring your Pure Heart Simple Mind experience, and that in some small way this book has added to the quality of your life.

All the stories in this book, were originally published in my complimentary newsletter. So if you would like to stay in touch and read more, you are welcome to subscribe! You can find the Seishindo website at **http://www.seishindo.org**.

On my website you will find numerous resources to help you live a more fulfilling life, and over time I will be creating new material to supplement the book. So please consider continuing to travel with me by joining the Seishindo community.

Before signing off, I would like to ask you once again, What is the common ground all human beings share? What are the hopes and fears we all live with? What can you do to help support and nourish the people you come in contact with?

All the best to you going forward. Please stay open to the many wonderful people and experiences that await you!

Charlie

"The Self is a circle, whose center is everywhere and whose circumference is nowhere."

~ CARL G. JUNG